Revolution from the Middle

By
Samuel Francis

Columns and Articles from
Chronicles, 1989-1996

Middle American Press

Permission has been granted by Chronicles *magazine and its editor, Dr. Thomas Fleming, to reprint the articles of which this book is composed. All the chapters of this book were originally published in* Chronicles; *all the dates of their publication appear at the end of each chapter.*

Revolution from the Middle
By Samuel Francis

Published by
Middle American Press
P.O. Box 17088
Raleigh, NC 27619

Contents

Preface

Revolution from the Middle represents a significant departure from the hackneyed and ideologically-driven political analysis that today is peddled with dreary regularity by both the Left and the Right. Unlike the resentful Left with its tiresome clamor for a bigger share of the U.S. Treasury, or the obsequious Right with its embarrassing corporate sycophancy, author Samuel Francis actually defends and advocates the just interests of the core population of his own country.

Such a stance is unique among modern American political writers, and virtually absent among the programs and platforms of a broad spectrum of political parties and organizations. Today, neither Left nor Right even pretends to speak for the broad mass of the American people. Instead, they offer only rigid ideologies or the private claims of special constituencies. The Left, once a proud advocate of economic justice for workingmen, has become merely a mouthpiece for — and the exclusive property of — the many aggressive anti-Western ethnic groups seething in the body politic. Perhaps sensing profound demographic shifts, the post-WWII Left gave up compassion in exchange for minority resentment. Dumping the West's workers, it picked up the cause of Third World immigrants and their craving for the benefits of the civilization that the Euro-American peoples created for themselves, from good housing and education to health care and welfare, as well as jobs and pensions. The Left no longer mobilizes for justice, but for booty. At the same time, the Right has proven itself unable to fulfill its historic role as conservator of the people's heritage, values, and traditions. Preferring economics to culture, the modern Right has transformed itself into a tiny band of pamphleteers and pundits who defend little else but multinational money-making. The cheap labor policies of giant corporations get considerable favorable attention in the pages of the mainstream Right's publications. But the mere mention of preserving America's cultural heritage is enough to send the editors ducking for cover.

The resulting political configuration of the late twentieth century has left Middle Americans stranded in a wasteland. Abandoned by the Left and Right, the broad middle classes of farmers, shopkeepers, housewives, laborers, small businessmen, engineers, and corporate office-workers are exposed and vulnerable. Without protection in the halls of government, they are targeted by elites for harboring "politically incorrect" thoughts, drafted to fight in international wars, and plundered to supply the wherewithal to keep the commercial multicultural system running.

But as Dr. Francis demonstrates in this fascinating collection of essays, Middle America is not asleep. Francis cites the recent insurgent political candidacies of Pat Buchanan and even Ross Perot as part of a growing body of evidence that a new consciousness is emerging in the heartland. Fed up with political and corporate elites hostile to their interests, Middle Americans are groping for new forms of political expression outside the traditional Democrat and Republican formulas. In recent decades, those formulas have only served the interests of entrenched elites who are able to divide their opponents into warring factions while the management of the parties remains safe in the hands of those who share a common globalist outlook in pursuit of free trade, open immigration, and the dismantling of the West's distinct cultural identity. As Middle Americans probe for cracks in the system, overwhelming majorities have passed state ballot initiatives for term limits, curbs on welfare for illegal aliens, and prohibitions against preferential government favors for homosexuals and racial groups, an unmistakable sign of the people's growing revulsion at the Byzantine ideological fetishism of America's political elites. Sledgehammer reactions by the federal judiciary in striking down those initiatives promise to exacerbate existing frustrations and highlight the growing ideological conflict between the people and those who rule them, perhaps triggering even more new adherents to the Middle American revolution.

That conflict is one of the reasons for the founding of *Middle American News* just about a year ago. Until it appeared, Middle Americans had few sources of news and analysis about their own political circumstances. A lively and independent political tabloid committed to no established interest group, its continuing success is perhaps still more evidence that one day soon a self-conscious Middle America will be standing on its feet to seize the reins of power. Distribution of this book by *Middle American News* may be evidence of that as well, representing perhaps a tentative manifesto of the basis for that revolution.

Steeped in the tradition of social analysis cultivated by Vilfredo Pareto, Gaetano Mosca, James Burnham, and others, Dr. Francis provides a refreshing and stunning theoretical dissection of contemporary political events that is unavailable elsewhere, and which is therefore all the more valuable. Even though no one can say for certain whether an insurgent Middle America will eventually free itself from the elite's predatory system, that triumph is certainly not possible without the efforts that this book and that of the readers of *Middle American News* represent.

In *The Ruling Class* Gaetano Mosca eloquently summarized the value of that work:

> Every generation produces a certain number of generous spirits who are capable of loving all that is, or seems to be,

noble and beautiful, and of devoting large parts of their activity to improving the society in which they live, or at least to saving it from getting worse. Such individuals make up a small moral and intellectual aristocracy, which keeps humanity from rotting in the slough of selfishness and material appetites. To such aristocracies the world primarily owes the fact that many nations have been able to rise from barbarism and have never relapsed into it. Rarely do members of such aristocracies attain the outstanding positions in political life, but they render a perhaps more effective service to the world by molding the minds and guiding the sentiments of their contemporaries, so that in the end they succeed in forcing their programs upon those who rule the state.

We cannot suppose that there will be any lack or deficiency of such generous souls in the generations that are now rising. But it has happened more than once in the long course of human history that the efforts and sacrifices of such people have not availed to save a nation or a civilization from decline and ruin. That has occurred, we believe, largely because the "best" people have had no clear and definite perception of the needs of their times, and therefore of the means best calculated to achieve social salvation. Let us hope that that clear perception will not be wanting today...

Jerry Woodruff
Editor, *Middle American News*

The author wishes gratefully to acknowledge the permission granted by *Chronicles* magazine and its editor, Dr. Thomas Fleming, to reprint the articles of which this book is composed. All the chapters of this book were originally published in *Chronicles*; all the dates of their publication appear at the end of each chapter.

Introduction:
The Long March of the MARs

Since 1989, I have been writing a regular column, "Principalities and Powers," for The Rockford Institute's monthly magazine, *Chronicles: A Magazine of American Culture*. These columns have centered around the social and political phenomenon that I have called the "Middle American Revolution," and those columns that in my view best reflect that theme are here collected and reprinted.

The Middle American Revolution is an extended process by which the group that sociologist Donald I. Warren in 1976 called "Middle American Radicals" (MARs) challenges the power of the established, mainly liberal, elites that have come to prevail in American public life, in politics, the economy, and the culture. Middle American Radicals are essentially middle-income, white, often ethnic voters who see themselves as an exploited and dispossessed group, excluded from meaningful political participation, threatened by the tax and trade policies of the government, victimized by its tolerance of crime, immigration, and social deviance, and ignored or ridiculed by the major cultural institutions of the media and education. In Professor Warren's original analysis, MARs were the backbone of George Wallace's national political following. They later supported Ronald Reagan and became known as the "Reagan Democrats." More recently, they have supported such "outsider" candidates as Ross Perot, David Duke, Ralph Nader, and Jerry Brown. In 1996, they began to receive national political attention, as *Newsweek* magazine dubbed them the "Radical Middle."

But the major national expression of Middle American Radicals thus far has been the presidential campaigns of Pat Buchanan in 1992 and 1996. Only Buchanan managed to capture the strange synthesis of right and left that characterizes the political beliefs of MARs — their combination of culturally conservative moral and social beliefs with support for economically liberal policies such as Medicare, Social Security, unemployment benefits, and economic nationalism and protectionism. Indeed, only Buchanan succeeded in coming close to formulating something like a new ideological identity in American politics with what he variously called his "new nationalism," "new populism," or "economic populism." Candidates like Brown and Nader remain too closely linked to the liberal establishment and its cultural radicalism to appeal to many MARs. David Duke's Ku Klux Klan coattails disturbed too many voters to allow him to break out of the ghetto in which he had isolated himself, and Ross Perot has persistently refused to embrace any of the moral and social issues that could gain him the allegiance of alienated socially conservative MARs.

Nevertheless, Buchanan failed to win the Republican presidential nomination, for essentially three reasons. In the first place, his campaign organization was underfunded and understaffed and was obliged to concentrate on the early primary contests like Iowa and New Hampshire. While Buchanan did well in these states, his campaign was not adequately prepared for the later contests that proved decisive. Second, though Buchanan began receiving favorable press attention in his second campaign in late 1995, as soon as he started showing that his campaign was a serious contender by winning early caucus votes and the New Hampshire primary, the national media launched what was perhaps the most intensely hostile blitzkrieg in American history. Given the transparent inaccuracy and blatant sensationalism of much of the reportage and commentary on Buchanan, it is difficult to avoid the conclusion that the blitzkrieg was a deliberately concocted propaganda crusade launched by the unofficial guardians of elite dominance in the media.

The third reason for Buchanan's failure lies in his decision to remain within the Republican Party. Not only did Buchanan as a Republican have to battle the well-constructed party machine of Bob Dole; but also the rise of "neo-conservatism" within the American right since the 1970s and the re-emergence of "centrist" Republicanism in such leaders and candidates as George Bush, Dole himself, Haley Barbour, and their allies means that the GOP has become too wedded to the established elites and has moved too close to its corporate sponsors to serve as a useful vehicle of Middle American revolt. Despite the Republican capture of both houses of Congress in 1994, the leaders of the party in Congress refused to put Middle American themes and issues on their agenda. They failed to end affirmative action or control immigration, even though opinion polls showed overwhelming popular majorities in favor of doing so. They supported President Clinton on globalist trade and foreign policy issues like NAFTA, the World Trade Organization, the Mexican Bailout, and military intervention in Somalia, Haiti, and Bosnia. Their "Contract with America" carefully avoided the more radical Middle American concerns and contented itself with essentially policy-wonk reforms to which most Americans were indifferent, and they managed to alienate Middle Americans by reckless libertarian rhetoric that chattered about reducing middle-class entitlement programs on which Middle Americans (especially the elderly) had become dependent. It is hardly surprising, then, that what has become the mainstream of the Republican Party and its leadership circles were even more savage in their denunciations of Buchanan than the liberal media.

Buchanan's decision to remain within the GOP and his effort to build a populist crusade around it were therefore probably doomed from the start, although his early victories and even his winning of some 35 percent of the primary vote in Rustbelt states like Ohio and Michigan showed that his message of populism, cultural traditionalism, economic nationalism, immigration restriction, and an "America First" foreign policy resonated with rank-and-file voters. The irony of the Republican primary campaign lay in early losers like Phil Gramm, Lamar Alexander, and Steve Forbes whining that Buchanan was too "extreme" and had no support, even as he consistently won more votes than they did.

Yet the Middle American Revolution is not merely a matter of politics and elections. In the last few years, there have been definite signs of the impending collapse of what was once known as the "national consensus," the "vital center," the "public philosophy," or other labels that purported that the beliefs and world view associated with a narrow band of elite publications, intellectuals, and politicians were really representative of what most Americans think and believe. This collapse is not merely a change of political opinions but resembles what historians and sociologists call a "paradigm shift," a major alteration in the basic assumptions about social and political life. Such conceptual pillars of the "vital center" as the faith that the national government is both honest and competent and can be trusted with vast power for the purpose of engineering progressive social reconstruction are now discredited. So is the myth that human beings are merely the products of their social and economic environment, an assumption that lay behind such liberal "experiments" as the New Deal, the Great Society, the War on Poverty, racial integration, and even many of the foreign policy adventures of the "imperial period" of American history from Woodrow Wilson's war "to make the world safe for democracy" to the "New World Order" of George Bush and Bill Clinton.

Finally, even the fundamental rationalism on which liberalism was founded and which sought to justify the faith that rationalistic planning and management of society and the economy could create utopian social progress is now withering. The revival of such movements as evangelical Christianity, "New Age" mysticism, occultism and UFO cults, the racial nationalism of the Nation of Islam and similar movements among non-whites, the popularization of conspiracy theories, the appearance of secessionist and separatist movements, and the emergence of "militias," "skinheads," and other sects and cults among whites that were once considered "fringe" suggest that the "vital center" has spun out of control.

What seems to be happening is what historians know as a "crisis of legitimacy," a period in which the subjects of a regime no longer believe in the claims of the regime to be legitimate, and this crisis is beginning to permeate and puncture not only the political culture but also the very cosmology on which the regime rests. Historically, such crises of legitimacy occur in the period just before a revolution, and all the major revolutions of modern history — in 17th century England, 18th century France, and early 20th century Russia — have been preceded by just such implosions of the belief systems on which the old regimes rested.

Yet few supporters of the Middle American Revolution advocate or believe in violent or illegal means to accomplish their ends, and as long as legal and democratic procedures for political and social change remain available, there is no reason why MARs should seek other avenues to power. It is also a feature of crumbling old regimes, however, that when their elites perceive that their ideologies and formulas are no longer credible to their subjects, they turn to repressive means to keep control. Today one thinks of Waco, Ruby Ridge, gun control laws, "counter-terrorism" laws, "hate crime" laws, "Political Correctness," unprecedented increases in government wiretapping and the number of police officers, the trend toward federal involvement in law enforcement, the use of the military for law enforcement purposes, and the enhancement of the powers of the FBI, the Drug Enforcement Administration, and the Bureau of Alcohol, Tobacco, and Firearms.

If the regime of the elites does turn toward repression in its effort to control and derail the Middle American Revolution, it will almost certainly fail and will succeed only in further alienating and radicalizing those who are already losing faith in their government, their economy, and their culture. It is vital to the success of that revolution that its adherents not succumb to "false consciousness" in the form of crackpot theories or violent remedies that at best accomplish nothing to advance serious Middle American goals and at worst play into the hands of their enemies. Whatever political leaders emerge to carry the banners of the MARs in the future and whatever forms Middle American political consciousness and activism take, Middle American Radicals can best push their cause forward by undertaking a "long march through the institutions" and silently building their own "counter-culture" or "counter-hegemonic force" that eventually will be able to challenge the existing regime of the elites and will "prefigure" the kind of new system they will construct. That kind of long march is by no means as glamorous as reckless rhetoric about "guerrilla warfare" and endless twaddle about vast and invincible conspiracies, but it will accomplish far more. As Middle Americans approached the end of 1996 with yet another election between two virtually indistinguishable presidential candidates who competed with each other only in bolstering the elite they both represented and in avoiding serious issues the elites do not want discussed, there was every sign that more Americans than ever before are ready to sign up for the long march to victory.

Toward a New Force

In the 1950s, American conservatives, subscribing to what Clinton Rossiter called a "thankless persuasion," were a hard-shelled, pig-eyed lot who took no prisoners and asked no quarter. *National Review*, in a once famous but now largely forgotten editorial in its premier issue, vowed that its mission was to stand athwart history and cry stop. Admittedly, this was hardly the most fetching advertisement with which to inaugurate a political and intellectual movement, but it reveals the grim mentality of the American right of that era.

In the 1980s, the new breed of conservatives, of whom Rep. Newt Gingrich and Housing and Urban Development Secretary Jack Kemp are representative, is at pains to distance itself from that mentality. Its exponents seize every opportunity to make known their differences with a school of thought and politics that scorned the enlargement of the state and the slogans of "mandate," "crusade," and "vision" that legitimized it. What is now somewhat deprecatingly called the "Old Right" despised the notion that the government should help redesign the society it was supposed to protect, expressed contempt for the utopian effervescence of progressivism, and espoused a deep loyalty to and affection for its country and the historic culture and people who defined the country.

What some are calling "progressive conservatism" parts company with the Old Right on all these fronts. Last winter, during a Republican strategy conference at which Mr. Gingrich and his court presided, the talk was all about how to sever whatever links remain between the conservatism of the past and the translucent future that the new Minority Whip wants to personify. "We're going to have to start talking, for example, about civil rights and affirmative action [to appeal to black voters] in ways that we haven't before and that may offend some conservatives," one "key conservative theorist" was quoted as saying. "We have to have a caring, humanitarian, reform Republican Party," said Mr. Gingrich himself, "that accepts the burden of being a governing conservatism, not just an opposition conservatism." "We have to get over the hump of being the parsimonious, anti-compassion, anti-humanitarian party which really doesn't care if people starve in the streets as long as the budget is balanced," said Republican strategist Jeffrey Eisenach, one of Mr. Gingrich's close advisers. "I never thought frankly," said New Right leader Paul Weyrich, "that I would sit in a Republican meeting and hear the terms 'crusade to save the children'."

Mr. Kemp too seems enthusiastic about the new role that the federal government will enjoy. Early in his brief-lived campaign for the presidency in 1987, Mr. Kemp promised that "'Getting the government off the backs of the American people' will be no one's slogan in 1988. Making government more efficient and more effective will be the thing this time. I've never understood why conservatives positioned themselves against government." Mr. Weyrich added, "the truth is that some of us believe in government activism.... too often, we have attempted to reject the obligation welfare represents, the obligation to the poor, the homeless, the unemployed and the disabled. ... We accept the obligation welfare represents."

The zest for government activism appears to be the center of the new vision prophesied by the triumvirate and its ideological outriders. That alone would dissociate it from the anti-statist conservatism of the past, but more is involved in the transfiguration of the American right than a mere tactical change of instruments by which its political leaders may work their will.

The changes in thought and rhetoric that distinguish the "progressive conservatism" of the triumvirate and its support-ers from its predecessors of the Old Right reflect a significant social and demographic transformation of American political culture. Whereas Old Right conservatism was by and large the expression of the interests, values, and aspirations of the American bourgeois elite, the triumvirate and its political formulas express those of a relatively new elite of urbanized, techno-cratic professionals who make their living and gain power and status in mass organizations. This new "managerial" elite, as James Burnham called it, displaced the older bourgeoisie as the dominant force in politics, the economy, and culture in the early twentieth century. Between the Depression and the end of World War II it seized power at the national level and in the 1960s through the New Frontier and the Great Society em-barked on what it thought would be the final mop-up of its bourgeois rival.

The new elite found a rationale for its aspirations to power in the ideology of liberalism, which offered justifications for the enlargement of the state and its fusion with other mass or-ganizations — corporations and unions in the economy, mass universities, large foundations, and the mass media in the mana-gerial cultural apparatus. The cosmopolitan and universalist ethos of liberalism served to challenge bourgeois moral and social codes and attachment to local and national institutions, while liberal meliorism and progressivism legitimized the new elite's application of its technocratic and managerial skills to government, the economy, and society.

With the exhaustion and discrediting of liberal ideology in the 1960's and 1970's, however, the elite had to formulate a new ideology. This is where "progressive conservatism" comes in.

In the 1980s, the younger members of the managerial elite came to be known as "yuppies," and though they questioned many of the policies of New Deal-Great Society liberalism, they retained its cosmopolitan and essentially materialistic values and showed little hesitancy about using governmental power against social and cultural institutions to create "openness," "opportunity," and "democracy." They also became enamoured of new technologies that seemed to promise all sorts of secular salvations, from the end of war and poverty to the global unification of government and culture, and which offered endless frontiers for the utilization of their esoteric skills.

"Progressive conservatism" and its ideological siblings are designed to capture and mobilize the young (now tending toward middle aged) urban professionals of the managerial elite. The Republican Party may not need them to win elections — they have plain old Middle Americans, who have nowhere else to go, for that — but it does need them to govern. The federal government, the congressional staffs, and the think tanks and media institutions on which neo-conservatives and progressive conservatives depend simply can't operate without them.

The union of the Republican Party with the managerial elite and its apparatus in the government means the end of an era in American political culture. Since the New Deal, the Taft-Goldwater-Reagan wing of the Republican Party has preserved as a norm of American politics opposition to "big government" and the "rendezvous with destiny" that history had supposedly arranged for us. The articulation of that norm set an important boundary to the public discourse in which political issues were debated.

But now that kind of bourgeois conservatism and its determination to stop history and get off has become a moribund political and intellectual force, because the social formation that supported it and the values and interests of which bourgeois conservatism was an expression are extinct or dying. The "progressive conservatives" and their following come not to praise, let alone restore, the bourgeois order but to bury it; not to stand athwart history and cry stop but to clamber on board, toot the horn, and press the throttle full steam ahead. If there is to be any resistance to or restraint on the managerial state and its interminable war against what remains of American culture, it can come from neither the progressive conservatism of Mr. Gingrich and Mr. Kemp nor the bourgeois conservatism of the Old Right but from some new force that has not yet taken shape.

[August, 1989]

Left, Right, Up, Down

Since the time of the French Revolution, the labels "left" and "right" have served as universal symbols on the road atlas of modern politics. The exact meaning of the symbols has never been clear, especially when they are applied outside the narrow streets of practical politics and extended to the broader ranges of philosophy, religion, and even aesthetics. Nevertheless, like "A.M." and "P.M." or "A.D." and "B.C.," left and right have become indispensable to the mental and verbal organization of otherwise incomprehensible phenomena.

Because they originally pertained to the different sides of parliamentary assemblies in the wake of the French Revolution and served to distinguish those, on the left, who supported the revolution and its legacy from those, on the right, who opposed it, left and right might retain some clear meaning if employed in that sense. In so far as the ideological legacy of the revolution is captured in its motto of "Liberty, Equality, Fraternity," and in so far as contemporary politics still revolves around these terrible pleasantries, then we might continue to lump certain schools of politicians and political thinkers as "left" and others as "right."

But throughout the 1980s (and probably henceforward) such schools seem to be out for a long vacation. What is called the "right" in American politics today seems to invoke and take seriously all the slogans and cliches that derive from Liberty, Equality, and Fraternity and which would ordinarily locate their exponents on the left. Its champions talk of the "global democratic revolution," universal "human rights," "equality as a conservative principle," and the final emancipation of mankind from war, racial and national prejudice, tyranny, and poverty through universal economic and technological progress. No noble savage of Enlightenment lore nor his less noble descendants who pulled the ropes of the guillotine in the Year One would raise an eyebrow at the rhetoric and ideology of the contemporary American right.

Things aren't much different on what is called the "left." While once only rightish pessimists such as Spengler or Henry Adams talked about the decline, suicide, or dissolution of the West, today that theme is a staple on the rubber chicken circuit of liberal Democrats. Newly elected Democratic Majority Leader Richard Gephardt sounded the theme when his colleagues elevated him to his new post in the House, and last year he ran his presidential campaign on the issue of "economic nationalism," which Michael Dukakis also picked up when his own campaign ran into trouble. Whatever the economic merits of their ideas, that issue presupposes the reality and significance of national identity and contradicts the universalism implicit in the "Fraternity" that *sans culotte* armies spread across Europe in the 1790s.

Moreover, *Washington Post* columnist Richard Cohen, whose writings usually seem to be archetypal expressions of what the conservative collective unconscious wants liberals to say, recently penned a column that older conservatives ought to find unexceptionable. Mr. Cohen inveighed against the homogenization of America through shopping malls, fast food emporia, motel chains, housing developments, and "restorations" such as those in Williamsburg and Old Town in Virginia. The ideological premise of such homogenization, of course, is again the cosmopolitanism and universalism that informed the French Revolution and which liberated souls such as Mr. Cohen have trumpeted throughout their careers. Whether he has as yet grasped the contradiction between his recent column and his lifelong convictions I do not know.

One gentleman of the left who has grasped it, however, is the radical historian Christopher Lasch, whose recent writings reveal a profound suspicion of the abstractions that lurk in Liberty, Equality, and Fraternity. In a recent essay in the *New Oxford Review*, Mr. Lasch dwells on his intellectual autobiography, showing how his personal and intellectual development eventually led him to shatter the very idols of the left to which he had paid homage all his life. Noting that the left's own road map of America was divided between New York and Washington on the one hand and what it regarded as "the vast hinterland beyond the Appalachians — the land of the Yahoo, the John Birch Society, and the Ku Klux Klan" on the other, Mr. Lasch expressed his emerging disenchantment with the contours of that map.

> By the late 1970s and early 1980s I no longer had much confidence either in the accuracy of this bird's-eye view of America or in the progressive view of the future with which it was so closely associated. "Middle Americans" had good reason, it seemed to me, to worry about the family and the future their children were going to inherit. My study of the family suggested a broader conclusion: that the capacity for loyalty is stretched too thin when it tries to attach itself to the hypothetical solidarity of the whole human race. It needs to attach itself to specific people and places, not to an abstract ideal of universal human rights. We love particular men and women, not humanity in general. The dream of universal brotherhood, because it rests on the sentimental fiction that men and women are all the same, cannot survive the discovery that they differ.

Mr. Lasch's thoughts in this passage, one would think, would induce our keepers of the conservative flame to spread a feast of welcome for him. But don't unfold your napkin just yet.

Mr. Lasch neither calls nor thinks of himself as a conservative, and in that he is probably wise. Were he to do so, passages such as the one quoted above would be greeted with the most vituperative abuse from those who claim that title today. The self-appointed swamis of the right, from their yachts and Alpine retreats, would compare him to excrement, even as they perspired over the closing of the American mind and preached the virtues of pluralism. Cries of "anti-Semite," "xenophobe," "nativist," and even "agrarian" would pierce the walls of his study and silence his tergiversations on the subjects of progress and universalism. His academic career would be threatened by unsolicited phone calls to his dean from spiteful colleagues. The tories who prance through the parlors of Manhattan and Georgetown would make sedulous inquiry as to his thoughts during the civil rights movement while awarding bountiful grants to decrepit social democrats and second-rate defectors from SDS. Were Mr. Lasch to spread his sails to the winds from the American right today, he would soon find himself marooned in an archipelago of small towns, intact families, and agrarian communities far from the political sea lanes plied by the clipper ships of self-proclaimed "conservatives."

Alas, Mr. Lasch is not typical of the contemporary left, however, nor are the ruminations emitted by the estimable Cohen or the honorable Gephardt. Mr. Lasch is correct that the mainstream of left-liberalism in America today remains nearly comatose with dread of the mainstream of America itself. But the great fear on the left seems to be matched on the right by an almost equal aversion to the American heartland. The contemporary right by and large much prefers the piña coladas of the secularized, deracinated megalopolis of the Northeast and the California Fringe to the white lightning of the piney woods, the Rockies, and the Great Plains.

Today, the right talks and thinks like the left, and the left, sometimes, sounds like the right. That kind of confusion suggests that both labels have outlived their usefulness and ought to be put to sleep. They have become prisons that house so many different and conflicting forces that the interests, values, and aspirations incarcerated in them are unable to find coherent political expression.

The political conflict of the future is likely to be not on the horizontal plane between left and right but along a vertical axis: between a Middle American substratum, wedded to the integrity of a distinct national and cultural identity, on the one hand, and, on the other, an unassimilated underclass in alliance with an alienated and increasingly cosmopolitan elite that has subsumed left and right and shares more common ground with snappily dressed Soviet commissars and Japanese corporate executives than with farmers in Kansas, small businessmen in Ohio, union members in Detroit, or fundamentalists in Alabama.

That conflict, of course, is not new, and the American right has waxed fat and happy by claiming to represent one side of it. But today its enchantment with global democracy, a global economy, and a global culture that will displace national particularity render that claim transparently fraudulent. If the remaining nucleus of American civilization is to survive, it will have to find a new label by which to identify itself and new guardians to lead its struggle.

[September, 1989]

New Nationalism

If conservatives carried revolvers, they'd probably reach for them at the sound of the word "nationalism." Perhaps it's just as well they don't carry revolvers, since nationalism usually makes its appearance armed with considerably bigger guns. In the Europe of Metternich and Castlereagh, nationalism was the vehicle for the revolutionary destruction of dynastic and aristocratic regimes and the parent of all sorts of modern nastiness. "From the French Revolution," wrote the conservative Anglo-Polish historian Sir Lewis Namier, "dates the active rise of modern nationalism with some of its most dangerous features: of a mass movement centralizing and levelling, dynamic and ruthless, akin in nature to the horde."

American conservatives have never been much more enthusiastic about nationalism than their European counterparts. The opposition to ratification of the U.S. Constitution was led by country gentlemen who knew very well that Alexander Hamilton's national unification meant merely the consolidation of northeastern dominance over the states and their distinctive subcultures. For the first seventy years of the United States' lifetime, the main political conflict revolved around whether the nationalists of the Northeast would succeed in impressing their thumbprints on the wax of the new republic. That, as Richard Weaver saw, was the issue in Daniel Webster's debates with South Carolina's Sen. Robert Young Hayne, and the concrete meaning of Webster's "Liberty and Union" speech

28

was that the republic should be unified around the northeastern goals of economic expansion and national power.

As every schoolboy knows (or used to know, back when teachers told schoolboys about Abraham Lincoln), those goals eventually triumphed, and the "equality" that Lincoln and his supporters preached with their terrible swift swords was largely a mask for an orgiastic ethic of producing and consuming, the Great Barbecue that culminated only in the present century. In Lincoln's day and under his leadership, northeastern financial and industrial centers finally gained enough material power and resources to crush their rivals. It was neither patriotism nor piety that ultimately made the *unum* prevail over the *pluribus*, but the acquisitive habits that Lincoln's "equality of opportunity" rationalized and which modern advertising, credit instruments, mass media, and government-managed demand succeeded in creating.

Be all that as it may, the United States today is a unitary nation-state, as much as traditionalist conservatives may be loath to admit it. If you don't believe it, travel to a city other than the one in which you live. You will discover that just about any place you visit in the United States today looks almost exactly like the one you left. Fast food palaces, shopping malls, mammoth supermarkets, hotel chains, modern highway networks, office buildings, high rises, and parking lots now define the public orthodoxy of the nation. If you visit bookstores, look at television, go to the movies, or listen to music or the news in any American city, what you read, see, or hear will be very much the same as in any other city. On a recent visit to Atlanta, I listened to the local TV news. It was all about child abuse, drug busts, and local political corruption — exactly the same as in Washington. Only the street names had been changed, and not to protect the innocent.

National unification of the United States has meant the de-

struction of local and regional variations and their homogenization under a regime of centralized power — economic and
cultural as well as political. But homogenization doesn't stop
at the water's edge. The universalist and cosmopolitan formulas that justified national unification — equality of opportunity,
human rights, economic growth, and material progress — don't
distinguish beween one nation and another, and ultimately they
demand the abolition of national distinctiveness and identity
just as easily as they do the homogenization of subnational regional and cultural particularity. The forces that bring Ken-
tucky Fried Chicken to Nebraska and Nevada, disseminate the
political insights of Rivera and Donohue to housewives in
Wyoming, and decide how small businessmen in Birmingham
should provide for the safety and health of their workers also
will export such progress to the rest of the world. Indeed, the
logic of this century's technological unification, and the interests of the elites that created and run it, dictate that the unity of
the nation make way for the homogenization of the world.

The globalist dynamic is working itself out even now. The
September issue of *Scientific American* was devoted to the
topic of "Managing Planet Earth," and the thesis of Paul
Kennedy's *The Rise and Fall of the Great Powers*, that the
United States is in a condition of decline, is routinely exploited
to justify the management of decline so that the United States,
in Professor Kennedy's words, can "adjust sensibly to the newer
world order." Secretary of State James Baker and Mikhail
Gorbachev become almost weepy when they talk about the
"transnational issues" that will fill the diplomatic platters of the
future — arms control, conflict management, global environmental and economic policies, and, of course, drugs. American servicemen already are in South America to help its governments perform what ought to be entirely domestic law enforcement functions against the Medellin Cartel, itself a

transnational corporate state. Global democratization is only one part of the effort to envelop the entire planet in a post-industrial web that will strangle local cultural, economic, and political autonomy.

Some Americans, especially the cosmo-conservatives in Manhattan and Washington, may fantasize that globalization will yield another "American Century," with Yankee know-how tossing institutional and ideological candy-bars to fetching senoritas in the Third World. But blue-collar workers in Detroit and construction men in Texas probably have a better grip on the realities of globalization as they watch their own jobs disappear before Asian competition and illegal immigrants. Globalization doesn't mean that America will prevail, but that it will vanish among the electrons and laser beams by which the planet is to be held together, just as Midwestern small businesses and Southern family farms vanished into the financial and industrial grids of the nineteenth-century nationalists.

But compared to what globalism has in store for us, nationalism looks pretty good. If what remains of the Middle American nucleus of American culture is to survive, it will have to evolve a new nationalist consciousness capable of resisting the global managerial system and of challenging its domestic apologists. This means that the main instruments of globalization — the internationalization of domestic law and policy through gradual subordination to transnational organizations and treaties; the internationalization of the economy through free trade and investment; and the internationalization of the historic American population itself through mass immigration and the delegitimation of the European roots of its culture — have to be decisively repudiated.

It also means a radical rejection of what historically has been the basis of American nationalism — the cult of economic growth, material acquisition, and universal "equality of opportunity" — and its reformulation in a new myth of the nation as a distinctive cultural and political force that cannot be universalized for the rest of the planet or digested by the globalist regime. Finally, it means that Middle America, for once, will have to get its act together to challenge the power of the ideological globalists who now prevail in the nation as both the "left" and 'the "right."

"In every republic," wrote Niccolò Machiavelli, "there are two parties, that of the nobles and that of the people." The former "have a great desire to dominate, whilst the latter have only the wish not to be dominated, and consequently a greater desire to live in the enjoyment of liberty." In the American republic, the "nobles" have corresponded to the forces that sought the unification of the country under their own formulas of egalitarian and acquisitive nationalism and who now beat the drum for global homogenization. The "people" have consisted of those groups and sections that have resisted unification, that wanted only to be left alone, and who sought, as Weaver described Hayne's idea of freedom, "protection to enable him to enjoy things, not a force or power to enable him to do things."

But the mere "wish not to be dominated," as the anti-Federalists, the Confederates, the agrarian populists, and, most recently, the grassroots adherents of the New Right wanted, has not sustained their independence and freedom or the integrity of their cultural institutions. If what remains of such forces are serious about resisting being swallowed by the new transnational colossus, they will have to recognize that they can do so only by dominating — that is, by becoming "nobles" themselves, by uniting in a new Middle American nationalism, and by putting aside the divisions and distractions that have turned them into the victims of fortune instead of her master.

[December, 1989]

This Land Ain't Your Land

Despite the zipity-doo-dah rhetoric that many conservatives have spouted for the last decade, the United States in the 1990's will encounter challenges that neither the "right" nor the "left" is prepared to recognize, much less meet. The challenges go far beyond the "relative decline" that Paul Kennedy's *The Rise and Fall of the Great Powers* prophesied in 1988. Mr. Kennedy argued only that the United States would be unable to keep pace with the redistribution of economic power toward the Pacific Rim and the transfer of military might that will follow it. He never broached the much more serious threats that today signify the rapid unraveling of American society: high school and college students who don't know when Columbus discovered the New World and who think the slogans of Karl Marx are drawn from the U.S. Constitution; urban murder rates that even idiot savants would find difficult to calculate; drug wars fought with arsenals the Viet Cong would have envied; political corruption that makes the senators of ancient Rome look like Eliot Ness's picked men; and a population so frightened of thrift and sacrifice and so addicted to instant gratification that it often prefers foregoing reproduction altogether to the responsibility of bearing and raising children.

Yet these signs of moral and social decomposition are not as alarming as the prospect, celebrated vociferously by right and left alike, of the United States' speedy absorption into a transnational or global economy that threatens to extinguish American national and cultural identity itself. Ignorance, crime, corruption, and avarice are vices that can be cured, regardless of how drastic the medicine. The danger of economic globalism is that, like the AIDS virus, it destroys the very mechanisms that enable the patient to recover, even as it entices him into the illusion that the disease is harmless.

That illusion is the dream of universal material acquisition that has animated the consolidation of the American Republic into what may be called "MacNation," a colossal aggregate bound together not by any natural sense of historic community but through the artificial bonds imposed by bureaucratic routines and disciplines, corporate market strategies, mass media, and the mass collective channels in which millions of Americans move, work, play, eat, spend, vote, and communicate daily. Having broken down the institutional distinctions and regional diversity that once characterized the Republic and its cultural identity, the dream and its current material incarnation in economic globalism are now in the process of folding MacNation into MacPlanet.

Last March, the prominent Japanese economist and management consultant Kenichi Ohmae told an audience at Washington's Institute for International Economics that "national borders are disappearing," a development Mr. Ohmae welcomes, at least for other peoples' nations, even as traditional Japanese nationalism enjoys a renaissance. Many self-professed conservatives greeted Mr. Ohmae's prediction with hearty approval, and the *Wall Street Journal*'s Walter S. Mossberg reported on the appearance of conservative "one-worlders," "economists and academics who believe that in a global economy, with goods and especially capital surging across political borders, the economic fortunes of individual countries aren't important anymore."

But if national borders aren't important anymore, neither are trade deficits, or mass migrations, or even "national interests." The same logic that dismisses borders and populations as meaningful features of national identity also implies that the nation itself is an artificial abstraction that can possess no interests for which individual "citizens" (another artifice) should be expected to sacrifice. It's no accident that the "conservatives" who sing the progressive utopia of the global economy are usually the same ones who drool over a Wilsonian "global democracy" in place of concrete national interests as the proper goal of our foreign policy.

Indeed, the ideology of economic globalism logically involves a kind of social and political nominalism that denies any meaning to groups smaller than "humankind." Not only nations but also classes, ethnic groups, religious sects, local communities, and families are artificial identities that merely thwart the fulfillment of universalist, cosmopolitan, humanist perfection and which have about as much permanency as a group of Las Vegas poker players. Contemporary globalism, economic or democratist, right or left, has a remote ancestor in the ruminations of the ancient Stoics, who argued for a "city of the world" that would transcend city-states and empires. Closer relatives are the political fantasies of the Enlightenment and their Marxist derivative that "the international party shall be the human race." But whatever despots the universalist dream could inspire in earlier eras, only in this century has it been able to assume the technological and economic integument to put the flesh of power on its ideological bones.

The exponents of economic globalism defend it with the argument that foreign investments and free trade create new jobs and provide sources of capital otherwise unavailable for economic growth, that the technological and economic integration of the planet will engender peace, fraternity, and opportunity for all human beings, and that democracy and human rights will follow such growth and opportunity as the night the day. Even if a new generation of Japanese warlords should come to power, the globalists argue, it would be unlikely to bomb Pearl Harbor if the Japanese already own most of Hawaii.

Of course, if the Japanese already owned most of Hawaii, it would be problematical to what extent Hawaii could be said to be part of America anyway. And Japanese ownership of the pearl of the Pacific is not out of the question. Earlier last year, Honolulu Mayor Frank Fasi complained that Japanese purchases of $9 billion worth of real estate in the islands had caused the price of housing in his city to rise 50 percent between 1987 and 1989. "They're buying up our homes and farmland," the mayor said, "Many Hawaiians can no longer afford to live here." Foreigners, mainly Japanese, already own nearly 75 percent of the office space in downtown Los Angeles, up from 64 percent in 1988 and 51 percent in 1987. In the District of Columbia, foreigners own 23 percent of the office property; in Maine, 10 percent; and in Atlanta, 25 percent. In the Farm Belt of the continental United States, the Japanese bought up 218,000 acres of farmland in 11 months in 1988 and 1989.

Whatever the material advantages of allowing foreigners to buy up our land, close out our industries, steal our inventions, take over our jobs, and move into our country, the economic globalists seem oblivious to the non-economic implications of their ideology and its practical consequences for the independence and integrity of the nation and its culture. Their larger error consists in their adherence to an economic determinism that they are the first to denounce when it pops up among Marxists and other socialists. Globalists assume not only that economic motivations are the chief springs of human action, that the desire for and pursuit of wealth and economic opportunity are what all human beings at all times in all cultures and all countries are seeking, but also that economic considerations are paramount in evaluating social and political arrangements.

Those assumptions bring the globalists close to what both Albert Jay Nock and the German free market economist Wilhelm Röpke called "economism," the "incorrigible mania," as Röpke defined it, "of making the means the end, of thinking only of bread and never of those other things of which the Gospel speaks." Nock, a religious skeptic who was less concerned but no less knowledgeable about the Gospel, held that economism "interpreted the whole of human life in terms of the production, acquisition and distribution of wealth. Like certain Philippians in the time of St. Paul, its god was its belly."

A nation, or even a planet, that recognizes no god other than its belly will quickly start wallowing in the ignorance, crime, corruption, and avarice that today afflicts the United States, and it will find itself unable to free itself of them. "After wealth, science, invention, had done all for such a society that they could do," wrote Nock, "it would remain without savour, without depth, uninteresting, and withal horrifying."

What is horrifying about the planetary utopia the economic globalists envision is not so much the impoverishment that may yet be visited upon the United States as other nations, less enchanted by this dream of days to come, gain wealth and power at our expense, but that Americans, whether they gain or lose, will cease to be Americans at all and find themselves reduced to "resources," stripped of the distinctive set of norms that unite and identify them as a people and dispossessed even of the memory of how to make themselves one. As resources, they will become interchangeable parts in the global economic mechanism, and their functions in it can be performed just as easily (or better) by workers from Latin America, managers from Asia, or investors from Japan or Europe. If whatever remains of the Middle American core of the American nation and its civilization is to preserve itself from the dispersion and dispossession that the new global economy promises, it will have to assert its national identity and interests in economic no less than in cultural and political terms.

[January, 1990]

One World

E conomic globalism, beloved of the contemporary right, may be the major threat to the national and cultural identity of American civilization in the coming decades, but its logical counterpart is the political globalism, long beloved of the left, that marches under the banner of "one world." As the economic dependence of the United States on foreign trade, investment, and credit waxes, the political autonomy, legal sovereignty, and national independence of the country will wane. The architects of the new world order understand this, and they are quietly pushing a series of treaties, laws, and new international arrangements intended to diminish national independence and construct a transnational regime to which American laws, jurisidictions, and citizens will be subordinated.

The major achievement of political globalism in the United States in recent years has been the ratification of the "U.N. Convention on the Prevention and Punishment of the Crime of Genocide" and the enactment of implementing legislation by the U.S. Congress to bring federal law into conformity with the convention's terms. Largely forgotten until revived by Ronald Reagan on the eve of the 1984 presidential election, the genocide treaty originally provided for the trial and punishment of persons, including U.S. citizens, who were accused and convicted of the crime of genocide. American citizens, that is, could be extradited to foreign countries to stand trial for a crime unknown to their own laws until the treaty created it. "Genocide" under the original language of the treaty was so broadly defined as to be absurd. Telling Polish jokes might be construed as genocidal under its terms if they could be shown to cause "serious mental harm" to sensitive Polish egos.

Mainly through the efforts of Sen. Jesse Helms, the genocide treaty was amended and its most flagrant abuses neutralized before a Republican Senate adopted it. In 1988 the Congress passed legislation that puts the treaty into effect and creates the new crime of "genocide" for the first time under U.S. law. Regardless of the changes the Senate approved, however, the principle of the treaty remains as obnoxious and harmful as ever, enacting the fundamental premise of political globalism that the domestic laws of a nation must yield to conventions passed by other states or by international organizations.

One of the major reasons there was any conservative opposition to the treaty at all was the concern about its effects on the state of Israel, which treats Palestinians in a way that might plausibly be interpreted as genocidal under the most generous reading of the definition contained in the treaty. I know of one conservative aide in the Senate who actually checked with the Israeli embassy to find out if it was all right for her and her principal to oppose the pact. Concern for the security of an ally is of course a legitimate reason to adopt or oppose a proposed act of statecraft, but it would have been refreshing if conservatives in the 1980s could have mustered similar solicitude for the fate of their own country as well.

Reliance on the treaty-making powers of the Constitution to change domestic laws is an old and favored trick of the one-world lobby, and it was to squelch such tricks forever that Sen. John Bricker sponsored his famous Bricker Amendment in the 1950s. The measure would have restricted the treaty-making powers of the president and was a favorite hobby horse of conservative statesmen well into the 1960s. Unfortunately, they failed in their efforts, and today with Republicans and conservatives embracing virtually unrestricted presidential power in foreign policy, we may soon expect to see some of the worst nightmares of Sen. Bricker and Robert A. Taft take flesh and come to life. The executive branch and its diplomatic bureaucracy in the State Department are already pushing several treaties that bind or alter U.S. domestic laws — on labor relations, torture, human rights, and other subjects of intense emotional appeal and closely connected to the internal institutions and legal preferences of this or any other country.

But nothing offers more opportunities for one-worldist mischief than environmentalism. Since the "environment" obviously extends across national borders, managing it cannot be restricted to a single state and has to be undertaken by several governments. The result of the "global environmental crises" now routinely discovered every year will be the regulation of the social, economic, and political life of particular nations in accordance with environmental rules promulgated (and presumably enforced) by a supra-national authority.

Writing in the lead article of *Scientific American*'s September, 1989 issue devoted to the topic of "Managing Planet Earth," William C. Clark of Harvard's Kennedy School of Government announced that one requirement for "adaptive planetary management" is:

> the construction of mechanisms at the national and international level to coordinate managerial activities. ... In fact, a dozen or more global conventions for protection of the environment are now in effect. ... [But] the immediate need at the international level is for a forum in which ministerial-level coordination of environmental-management activities can be regularly discussed and implemented, much as is already done for international economic policy.

The kind of transnational management of the natural environment that Mr. Clark advocates would indeed complement the similar arrangements already in place for global economic management. As libertarian Llewellyn H. Rockwell, Jr. recently pointed out, "Under the aegis of the Bank for International Settlements ... banking is now regulated on a global basis. And the Bush administration is pushing for world regulation of the stock, bond, and futures markets. The administration is also promoting — with the other G-7 industrialized nations — international cash controls, international financial police, international tax collusion, international fiscal controls, and a UN treaty to make confidential banking a crime."

If global management of the environment doesn't polish off the nation-state, managing the global economy certainly will. *New Republic* senior editor Robert Wright, in a recent essay in explicit defense of one-worldism, argues that global economic interdependence and the resulting "policy coordination" are pressures for the kind of "institutional subordination of national autonomy to international will" that he envisions for the planet of the future. "As the leaky national economy becomes hostage to international forces," he writes, "we can either seize control of these forces in concert with other nations, or surrender a good measure of control altogether."

The obvious, but seldom asked, question, of course, is: "who is 'we'?" Those who will gain from the evanescence of the nation-state and of the concept of nationality itself will be those elites able to preserve and enhance their own power in the new, denationalized order that the globalists anticipate — those who will be managing the environment, planning and running the world economy, and enacting, administering, or enforcing the transnational laws and treaties by which the planetary regime is to be governed and the human proclivity to differentiate into distinct groups restrained. The cultures, religions, languages, and nations from which this elite emerges will be largely irrelevant to its powers and interests. They will in fact present an obstacle to the furtherance of its powers and interests and will therefore need to be reduced or eliminated entirely if the emergent transnational managerial elite is to flourish. The elite may retain some quaint vestiges of nationalism, just as we today conserve places like Williamsburg, and it may even find nationalist imagery useful in gaining the confidence of patriotic types who fail to see the glories of the new age. But whatever the merits of the globalist argument that the world had just better get itself together or else face disaster, the logic of the new elite's interests will increasingly ensure that nationality — and the legal and political claims and cultural identities that go with nationality — is extinguished and its own global technocratic regime perpetuated.

Americans, who began their national history by severing the bonds that connected them to a dying civilization and who ventured into history determined to build a new civilization politically independent of and culturally unique among the powers of the earth, will find themselves reduced in both power and identity by the emergent world order that both the "right" and the "left" today like to celebrate. They will eventually find themselves delivered back to the mercies of whatever glorified pencil-sharpeners from Europe or the Third World happen to be in charge of their future this year, and they may become indistinguishable from the rest of the cattle in the global barnyard who provide the fluctuating, mobile populations of the planetary economy and government. Americans who don't want to become such cosmopolitan coolies need to start thinking about what they can do to preserve their nation, its heritage, and themselves from the managerial colossus that now begins to straddle the globe.

[February, 1990]

The New Underclass

L ike Satan in Dante's Inferno, the forces threatening the integrity of the American nation and its culture have three faces. The "global economy" and political one-worldism jeopardize the historic character, independence, and the very sovereignty of the United States. The third threat, the mass immigration that this country has endured for the last fifteen years or more, is no less a danger to the cultural norms by which American civilization has identified itself throughout most of its history. Nevertheless, like the internationalization of our economy and government, the internationalization of our population is consistent with the interests of the elites that welcome and encourage it.

Some 600,000 legal immigrants and refugees and as many as 1 to 2 million illegal aliens enter this country every year, most of them from Third World countries as different from the United States as the tatoos of the Jivaro Indians are from the painting of Rembrandt. Actually, no one knows how many illegal aliens are here. Some experts guess as many as 10 million. The *New York Times* reports the presence in the United States of some 20 million Mexican nationals whom the Mexican government is trying to manipulate to influence U.S. foreign policy. Most authorities now acknowledge that the immigration to this country in the last decade rivals the size of the last inundation of the late nineteenth and early twentieth centuries.

Americans who live on the periphery of the United States in the east, south, or west are familiar with the commonplace results of the invasion: clerks, waiters, and cab drivers who can't speak English and can't make change in dollars and cents; stores, churches, and whole shopping districts where the signs are in languages or scripts that most of us can't even identify, let alone read; and entire neighborhoods of men and women who dress, look, and sound like the extras in *Casablanca* or *A Fistful of Dollars*. But these are mainly just irritants. Eventually they will be resolved as the newcomers and their children are "assimilated" — i.e., pick up televisionese and adopt the sartorial splendors of K-Mart in place of their customary beach towels and pajamas.

When defenders of mass immigration talk about "assimilation," that's the kind they usually mean. Unfortunately, it doesn't help, unless you believe (as many defenders of mass immigration do believe) that American culture consists merely in what can be purchased at the nearest shopping mall. But Third Worlders who eat at McDonald's and wear Adidas T-shirts are no more real Americans than a nineteenth-century British proconsul who bought his daily bread at an Indian bazaar was a Hindu.

Those who believe a deeper American culture still exists and ought to be conserved (they used to be called "conservatives") have good reason to worry that the new throngs of foreigners among us will not assimilate to it in any enduring way. Not simply language and clothing but also less tangible qualities such as the unspoken assumptions of political culture, art and literature, entertainment and religion, education, morals, the family, and concepts of work and property together create the set of common norms by which Americans know themselves to be different from Canadians, Mexicans, Europeans, and other cultures. Those who ignore such cultural particularities or deny they exist will readily believe that immigrants from across the globe can become Americans in pretty much the same way that Pepsi Cola can market its products in Asia and Africa. But the process of becoming a real member of a living society is somewhat more complicated than translating advertising slogans into Japanese or Swahili.

It is especially complicated when, as today, there are major obstacles to assimilation. Sociologist Nathan Glazer, a supporter of immigration, points out that the discrimination and prejudice that in earlier eras helped accelerate the acculturation of new immigrants is today largely illegal. Civil rights legislation, equal opportunity codes, and court decisions have weakened the power of private and social institutions, no less than that of public authorities, to induce immigrants to conform to American norms. Today's "cultural authorities" legitimize and instigate "alternative life styles," eschew stereotypes, scorn WASP ethnocentrism, and indulge every known form of deviation and idiosyncrasy from the religious exotica of Santeria to the perversions of the National Man-Boy Love Association. Restaurants where once only the coated and tied dared enter now beg their customers to wear shirts and shoes. "Popular opinion," writes Mr. Glazer, "now questions the legitimacy and desirability of forcefully imposing a common identity on immigrants and members of minority groups."

But it's less "popular opinion" perhaps than the interests of the elites that run the country and refuse to take the minimal steps to restrict immigration, which actually serves to enhance their power even as it promotes the decomposition of a common culture. The uses to which the millions of new immigrants may be put go well beyond the cheap labor they provide to Western agribusiness and Southern construction firms.

The elites that prevail in the United States today are bureaucratic and technocratic, gaining power by their ability to manage and manipulate social change through the fused apparatus of the state, the economy, and cultural organizations in the form of mass media, foundations, schools, and churches. In the past, these elites have been able to ally with the American underclass — first, with the industrial working class in the early twentieth century; more recently, with the urban black lumpenproletariat — to dislodge rival elites in private, social, and local institutions and jurisdictions and to exploit the middle class. But as the underclasses of the past graduate to middle income status, the elites need new proletarians as allies to help sustain their dominance.

Third World immigration allows for the importation of a new underclass and provides unglimpsed vistas of social manipulation in the form of new opportunities for managing civil rights, ethnic conflicts, education, health, housing, welfare, social therapy, and assimilation itself. In 1988, state officials in California were bickering over who would control their state's 55 percent of $3.4 billion in federal aid intended as welfare, education, and health care aid for immigrants; and other states also were contending for their fair share of the booty. Last year, the *New York Times* reported, "Two recent surveys of newly legalized immigrants in California have found such low levels of education, employment and fluency in English that. . .current levels of federal and state assistance will be inadequate for them." Nor, of course, will they be adequate for the politicans and bureaucrats who can expect to administer the funds and run the programs.

Government elites thus anticipate using immigration as a new fulcrum of bureaucratic power, and they will have allies in other elites, public or private, that can advance their own agenda of managing social change and displacing traditional cultural institutions through the care and feeding of immigrants. "Hate crime" laws, racial sensitivity courses, and anti-Western Third

World curricula are among the instruments for imposing a new cosmopolitan cultural hegemony and plowing under Euro-American patterns of culture.

In Washington, a private foundation, the International Counseling Center, thrives on providing psychotherapy and counseling to Third World immigrants apparently driven to the brink of madness by their encounter with American civilization. The center also offers what it calls "cultural awareness training programs" to social service workers, school guidance counselors, corporate executives, and local government officials who have to deal with immigrants. The idea seems to be that if the aliens don't adapt to American folkways, the folkways must adapt to the aliens. Local "fire and rescue squads," says center associate Linda Camino, an anthropologist, "are called upon to supply services to a culturally diverse population. Cultural misconceptions [among the Americans thus "called upon"] can be insidious and can lead to unwanted outcomes."

One "unwanted outcome," also useful to American elites, is the political exploitation of the immigrants, legal or not, who constitute a new electorate as well as a new underclass. Liberal Democrats are demanding "instant voter registration" laws, to be enforced and supervised by federal officials against local and state jurisdictions, that are thinly disguised mechanisms for allowing illegals to cast ballots. The proposal was imbedded in the 1988 Democratic platform — this explains why Michael Dukakis and Lloyd Bentsen went around chattering in Spanish all the time — and is currently being peddled in the Senate by California Sen. Alan Cranston, who stands to benefit from the alien vote. But Republicans are not far behind, and in 1988 neo-conservative idol Jack Kemp gaily predicted that "in 10 years, one-quarter of the Republican Party will consist of conservative blacks, conservative Hispanics, conservative Asian-Americans — or else the Republican Party will resign itself to permanent minority status." Which party will take care of traditional Americans no one seems to know, or care.

Mass immigration is also perhaps the most useful instrument by which the very idea of nationality can be liquidated, and it thus fits well with the forces of economic and political globalism and with the interests of the emerging transnational elite, into which our own technocrats are fusing. As national populations and the cultures they carry become interchangeable through migration, the concrete meaning of citizenship, political loyalty, sovereignty, and other elements of nationality will yield to a new supranational regime over which the emergent elite presides.

Caught between the new underclass and the new elite, plain old Americans can look forward to subsidizing through their taxes not only their own cultural dispossession but also the eventual disappearance of the nation itself, to the advantage of an elite that has disengaged itself from the body of the society it manages. If the Americans at the heart of that body are serious about preserving their nation and their culture, they will have to escape from the vise the new elite and the new underclass have constructed by freeing themselves from the newcomers above and below them.

[March, 1990]

The Middle American Proletariat

It is hardly an accident that the decomposition of the American nation and its culture is paralleled by the decomposition of the American middle class. In the nineteenth century, nationality and the middle classes were born together as Siamese twins, and their enemies understood their linkage and tried their best to strangle them in their common cradle. They failed, and the twins grew up as inseparable companions. It therefore makes sense that they remain united in death as they were in life.

In American as in European history, the middle class was the creator and carrier of nationalism, so much so that a cliche common among historians and sociologists holds that in the United States the middle class includes everyone. Of course it doesn't, and didn't; but the epoch that historian John Lukacs calls the "Bourgeois Interlude" — from 1895 to 1955 — remains even today the normative period of American history, the era that bred the culture and character that most people, Europeans as well as Americans themselves, still think of as typically American, against which we still measure our achievements and failures.

But as Professor Lukacs notes, "middle class" and "bourgeois" are not the same thing. The former refers to a merely economic category that happens to enjoy a material income between that of the poor and that of the wealthy. A middle class is as logically necessary to social existence as the obverse of a coin is to its reverse. But the "existence of the bourgeoisie," writes Professor Lukacs, "has been a particular phenomenon, a historical reality." The principal characteristics of the bourgeoisie were not economic but cultural and psychic — "the sense of personal authenticity and liberty, the desire for privacy, the cult of the family, permanence of residence, the durability of possessions, the sense of security, and the urbanity of the standards of civilized life." They derived from or were associated with the bourgeois attribute of "interiority," a preoccupation with the self manifested in literature and the arts through the novel, the portrait, the keeping of diaries, and the publication of letters, and appearing socially and politically in the creeds of individualism and the self-determination of nations.

The life dates Professor Lukacs gives for the Bourgeois Interlude (1895-1955) identify the era's cultural personality, but the hegemony of the bourgeoisie in culture followed its economic and political triumph in the American Civil War by about 30 years, just as its demise in the mid 1950s followed by about 25 years its political and economic overthrow in the Depression and New Deal. In the pre-bourgeois period of American history, during what might be called the "First Republic," neither nationalism nor the bourgeois psyche prevailed, and a decentralized constitutional and social order prevented the consolidation of power by either the bourgeois capitalism of the Northeast or the aristocratic capitalism of Southern plantation masters.

The "Second Republic," the political expression of the Bourgeois Interlude, emerged from the Civil War and made the United States a singular noun and a real nation-state, just like Napoleon III's France or Bismarck's Germany. Bourgeois economic, political, and cultural dominance meant that the new elite no longer had to be content with patching up its own psychic interior. Now it could redecorate the souls of Southerners, Indians, Latin Americans, Filipinos, European dynasts, and anyone else whose spiritual architecture failed to meet bourgeois standards. The technology, industry, urbanization, and mass educational and communications institutions that the new bourgeois elite set up enabled it to start straightening out regional and social bumps in the road of progress within the United States and to make preparations for turning the rest of the world into a bourgeois parking lot.

In the process, the bourgeois elite generated its own destruction. Its corporations, banks, and universities and its pubescent bureaucracies gave birth to a new class of technocrats who had little use for bourgeois beliefs and institutions. In the economy, the "separation of ownership and control" removed bourgeois property-holders from the direction of their own firms and empowered professional managers in their place. In the state, democratization served to disperse sovereignty among the newly enfranchised and politically active masses, with the result that the "people" received the name of power but the experts who managed the state held its substance. Culturally, the new intelligentsia that crept out of bourgeois universities and into tenured chairs and the editorial offices of newspapers and magazines despised the bourgeois class that had created and subsidized it, and the new savants knit their brows to devise ways to humiliate, subvert, and overthrow the bourgeois order. All that was really necessary to accomplish that goal was for the new elites in the economy, state, and culture to meet, marry, and set up housekeeping, which they did with the blessing of progressivist ideology and an ample dowry from their new federal godfather.

By the end of World War II, the bourgeois class had been effectively decapitated as the dominant minority in the United

States or had been subsumed into the new managerial elite that now prevailed. No fratricidal conflict marked the transition from the Second Republic to the managerial imperium because the bourgeois elite, contemplating its interior navel, never fully grasped what was happening and was unable to muster the will or the temperament to resist it. Having insisted on wrecking the First Republic and reconstructing it to its tastes, the bourgeois elite lacked the capacity to preserve its own power or the national culture its power had created. In the end, its members lost only their dominance and not their fortunes or their heads, and there is no good reason for most Americans today to lament its passing.

But there is good reason to mourn what will befall those millions of Americans who were never part of the bourgeois elite but who formed their lives around bourgeois culture. As the managerial successors to the bourgeoisie push the United States into a new transnational order and ally with the underclass, the American middle class is being crushed between them and stripped of its cultural identity and heritage.

The end of the bourgeois order in the middle of the century transformed the American middle class from a bourgeois *Mittelstand* to a post-bourgeois proletariat. As political scientist Andrew Hacker describes this "new middle class," it is considerably larger than the old and hence is "unwilling and unable to adhere to rules tailored for a quite different group of individuals in quite different settings." It differs from the old middle class also in its high degree of transiency and mobility, its "national" rather than its local character, and its lack of property. While the new middle class glories in its affluence and ability to consume whatever managerial capitalism sets before it, it conspicuously lacks the material independence of the old middle class and the authority, security, and liberty that independence yields. The members of the new middle class, writes Mr. Hacker, "are employees, and their livelihoods are always contingent on the approval and good will of the individuals and organizations who employ them. ... Whatever status and prosperity today's middle-class American may have is due to the decision of someone to hire him and utilize his services."

Masticated by the Depression and World War II and digested by the mass organizations that swallowed the more compact bourgeois institutions, the American middle class has suffered a profound dispossession, regardless of the number of credit cards it carries. Alienated from the nation's past by its size and rootlessness, it retains only a fragmented memory of and identity with the historic national experience. Lacking the autonomy of the bourgeois middle class, it is unable to formulate a new identity that would offer resistance to the emerging transnational elite and its allies in the underclass. "In fact," writes Mr. Hacker, "the new middle class has many attributes in common with the traditional conception of a proletariat."

In the emerging global managerial regime, the middle class may soon be reduced to the other attributes of a proletariat as well. "By any measure," the *Wall Street Journal* reported in 1987, "the share of households with middle-class incomes has steadily declined"; the "once-tightly knit group has broken apart" and its "broad consensus on how to live and what constitutes success. . .has given way to an increasingly fragmented array of life styles and values." The need for wives and mothers to work to sustain middle class incomes and living standards weakens family bonds. Middle class home ownership is already obsolescent in many urban areas, and the violence of the underclass, domestic or imported, is abetted by the elite and drives the middle class from the cities their forebears built.

In Detroit, where nearly 10 per cent of the population has left since 1980, only two building permits for single family

homes were issued in all of 1987, and the Catholic archdio-
cese announced the closing of 43 churches in the city in
1988. During the Hundred Years War in Europe, wolves
roamed the streets of medieval Paris; today ring-necked
pheasants strut through the abandoned lots and buildings of
Detroit, keeping company with the human wolves who have inherited the city that put America in the driver's seat. In Los Angeles, reports the *New York Times*, "the exodus of white middle-
class residents began at least a decade ago. . .but recent alarm
over smog, gang violence, traffic and housing costs appears
to have accelerated the trend." More than 282,000 Californians moved out of the state entirely in 1988-89. "My 9-
year-old daughter comes home from school and says a class-
mate is dealing drugs," 29-year-old Carol Woolverton told
the *San Francisco Examiner* last July, "And there've been
so many kidnappings." She is reported to have moved to
Oregon with her husband, three children, and two pets.
Where will they run next?

Without the cultural cohesion that the bourgeois elite
imposed, the new middle class cannot expect to retain for
long its traditional identity and values, let alone its political
and economic power. But the new proletariat is no longer
part of a bourgeois social and political order; it is only an
artifact or remnant of it, and it cannot look to the bourgeois
elite for leadership or salvation. That elite is extinct, and
the national republic it governed during the Bourgeois Interlude is defunct along with it. If the post-bourgeois middle
class seriously wishes to avoid its own extinction, it will
have to evolve a new group consciousness and a new identity independent of both the moribund bourgeois elite and
the techno-bureaucracy of the global managerial order. It
will have to expurgate the self-indulgent "interiority" that
ultimately proved lethal to the bourgeoisie, and it must as-

pire to form the core of a new political and cultural order in which it can assert its own hegemony.

[April, 1990]

Life on MARs

After two years of desperate pretense that the Bush administration is but the long afternoon of the Reagan era, many of Mr. Bush's conservative supporters now begin to suspect that morning in America is fast lurching toward chaos and old night. The president's apparent willingness to consider tax increases, despite his best known campaign promise, and the return of Secretary of State James Baker from Moscow last spring wearing little more than his underpants have disabused many on the right of any illusions they may have harbored. They are late, but they are not alone, and far from the Beltway comes the unsettling murmur of rebellion, this time not from the tenured revolutionaries of the left or the tax-exempt populists of the right, but out of the swamps and hills of the American heartland.

When David Duke announced in 1988 that he would run for the Louisiana state legislature, few paid much attention. Mr. Duke first gained national headlines in the early 1970s, when he won fame for being a member of the Ku Klux Klan as well as a college graduate, and he has run for office several times before — most recently for president in 1988. Any almanac will give you a complete list of such also-rans, from anti-Masons and Know-nothings down to the candidacies of Angela Davis, Dr. Spock, and Lyndon LaRouche. But then Mr. Duke won the legislative race, the almanacs had to be re-written, and ears, even inside the Beltway, began to prick.

Mr. Duke not only won his election — against the brother of a former governor and despite the fulminations of President Bush and Republican National Committee Chairman Lee Atwater and the avuncular counsel of Ronald Reagan — but also now seems to be on the verge of trouncing Republican state Sen. Ben Bagert in Louisiana's senatorial primary next month. If, as seems likely, Mr. Duke beats Mr. Bagert and keeps Democratic incumbent Bennett Johnston from winning more than 50 per cent of the vote, he will face Sen. Johnston in November. Should he win against him, the rebellion will begin to sprint.

Mr. Duke, however, has come a long way since he posed for pictures in Klan robes and Nazi uniform. While he refuses to denounce the Klan, he does not spend time or energy arguing that God has cursed the children of Ham or that the Elders of Zion are fluoridating the drinking water from their headquarters in the Federal Reserve system. Nor does he dote on the conclusions of researches conducted by the late William Shockley, Arthur Jensen, and others who believe that human intelligence is largely inherited and that white people generally got a larger slice of the intellectual pie than black people. Just because he doesn't talk about such matters does not mean that Mr. Duke doesn't believe them, and he is quite cagey about whether he does or doesn't. But regardless of what he thinks about these and other subjects, Mr. Duke's success in the polls has little to do with such beliefs or with the kind of clothes he used to wear. Louisiana and most other states are full of characters who wear all kinds of funny uniforms and would like to have lots of political power, but few citizens there or anywhere else are dumb enough to vote for them.

Mr. Duke has gained and kept a political following because he understands something most contemporary conservatives have forgotten or in some cases never knew: What attracts voters to a candidacy of the right is not what the candidate thinks or says about the gold standard, creating democracy in Afghanistan, expanding economic opportunities, or being kinder and gentler, but what he will do to preserve and protect what used to be called the American Way of Life, the normative patterns and institutions that define and distinguish what Americans believe and do from what other peoples believe and do — in short, the American culture.

Voters — not all of them, but many — are attracted to candidates who express clear positions supportive of traditional American culture because they have to live every day with the cultural erosion spawned by politically engineered assaults from individuals and groups that despise American culture and want to get rid of it. For example, the ACLU and kindred lobbies that manipulate judicial power to uproot folkways and the distribution of social and political power that folkways support; the "multiculturalism" lobby, which uses the government education system to crush Euro-American culture and subordinate it to its own Third-World-Marxist-feminist-homophile superstitions; and the civil rights establishment and its allies in the immigration lobbies, which seek to dig a bottomless pit of welfare rights, political privilege, affirmative action programs, and set-asides to dispossess white Americans economically, politically, and culturally and gain the loyalty of their non-white following in the black underclass and the government-created middle class. Such forces also enjoy the support or acquiescence of the bureaucratic elites in the managerial state, corporations, unions, and mass media, which use them to expand their own power.

The practical results of the success of this alliance are commonly known in the forms of violent crime that crippled police and prosecutors are unable to suppress, of entire systems of local government overturned by courts for the purpose of ensuring "minority" power, of competent white students denied admission to college because of the lower standards of enrollment universities allow for non-whites, and of qualified white job applicants unable to work because of affirmative action and set aside plans. Yet such material consequences of the racial and cultural revolution merely frame its substance. In high school and college, television and film, the traditional culture of Europe and America is vilified, belittled, debunked, and deconstructed, while white, Christian, male heterosexuals are consistently portrayed as criminals, tyrants, incompetents, and madmen. Probably more than the direct material effect of dispossession, this less tangible but far more pervasive dismantling and discrediting of an entire civilization has produced the smoldering psychic embers from which rebellion bursts into revolutionary flame.

The core of the revolution consists in what sociologist Donald I. Warren some 16 years ago called "Middle American Radicals," or "MARs," a social and political force largely identical to what is usually called — depending on one's inclination to affect dispassion, enthusiasm, or contempt — "lower middle class white ethnics," the "Reagan Democrats," or the "Bubba vote." Professor Warren, however, defined MARs in terms of a common attitude they shared. "MARs are a distinct group," he wrote, "partly because of their view of government as favoring both the rich and the poor simultaneously. . . MARs are distinct in the depth of their feeling that the middle class has been seriously neglected. If there is one single summation of the MARs perspective, it is reflected in a statement which was read to respondents: *The rich give in to the demands of the poor, and the middle income people have to pay the bill.*"

The white voters who elected Mr. Duke to the state legislature last year from District 81 are virtual MARs archetypes. According to a survey conducted for the *New Orleans Times*

Picayune after the election,

> Duke's constituents live in a microcosm of white, suburban America. District 81 is characterized by middle incomes, fear of crime and a distaste for taxes. Moreover, the voters ... express a smoldering [there's that word again] sense that, at worst, government confiscates the work of its best citizens and lavishes it, to no apparent effect, on people who are ungrateful or openly hostile.
>
> Affirmative-action programs, minority set-asides, racial quotas and other efforts on behalf of blacks have tilted the system against them, the voters said. When it comes to job and educational opportunities, they feel whites increasingly are ending up on the short end of the stick.

In Duke, voters said they saw an opportunity to fight back. Voters won't get that opportunity from Mr. Bush, however, nor from Dan Quayle, Jack Kemp, Newt Gingrich and the other luminaries of the Republican firmament, nor even from their ideological mentors who shine under the labels of "neo-conservatism," "big government conservatism," "cultural conservatism," and, most recently, "the New Paradigm." Last summer the Heritage Foundation published a report on the Kennedy-Hawkins Civil Rights Bill of 1990, and while Heritage properly opposed the bill and affirmative action, it pronounced what is nothing less than an abandonment of traditional conservative principle regarding civil rights legislation.

The "conservative view of progress" on civil rights, Heritage informed us, demands that "government must prosecute cases of discrimination against individuals to the full extent of the law. Title VII of the 1964 Civil Rights Act ... should be strengthened to include remedy of damages against those who wilfully discriminate. Building on this enforcement strategy, the conservative civil rights strategy would call for aggressive court and legislative action to challenge modern-day Jim Crow laws that stifle minority business development." Examples of such latter-day "Jim Crow laws" include "the 1931 Davis Bacon Act, which freezes out minority firms from government construction contracts, and onerous licensing laws for professions ranging from cosmetology to child care."

Yet these laws, as the Heritage paper acknowledges, are "seemingly neutral in their impact on the races," and, unlike Jim Crow laws, which explicitly discriminated on the basis of race, merely have the effect of placing black-owned firms under disadvantage. There are good reasons to repeal Davis-Bacon and many occupational licensing laws, but to do so because they have the effect — rather than the intent — of racial discrimination is to embrace conventional liberal ideas that legitimize affirmative action and special privileges for members of certain races over others. Through exactly the same logic, universities require lower SAT scores for black applicants than for whites because holding all applicants to the same standards, while "seemingly neutral," would in effect exclude many blacks from admission. Thus the new "conservative civil rights strategy" winds up in the same place conventional leftism started out.

Nor does Heritage explain why ending and punishing "racial discrimination" should be legitimate goals and activities of the federal government at all or why the state should undertake special efforts to ensure "business development" — or home-owning, or an end to poverty, or psychic contentment — for any particular group. Whatever the flaws of Jim Crow codes before the 1960s, federal involvement in chasing racial discrimination through the Civil Rights Act resulted in a massive expansion of centralized power on behalf of the therapeutic management of social, political, economic, and cultural relationships that no real conservative can countenance.

Heritage is not alone in demanding further acceleration of

the civil rights revolution through the use of federal power.
Last winter, conservatives gathered secretly in New York to
discuss what they were going to do with their little empires in
the coming decade. For "cultural conservative" Paul
Weyrich, the agenda seems to be focused mainly on helping
the black underclass. An eight-page memorandum circu-
lated by Mr. Weyrich at the meeting centered almost entirely on measures designed to help minorities in inner cities
while largely ignoring traditional white middle-class conservative constituencies on farms and in small towns and
urban neighborhoods that continue to face social, economic,
and cultural demolition.

Yet it is precisely such constituencies that supported conservative activism — indeed, made it possible through their
donations — and voted the current crop of Republican
politicoes into office. They did so because the propaganda
and rhetoric these activists and politicians uttered made them
believe that their interests would be defended and that the
continuing assault on their beliefs, life styles, institutions,
and aspirations would be resisted. But except for campaign
applesauce about Willie Horton, the Pledge of Allegiance,
the American flag, capital punishment, and religion, today's
"conservatives" have no serious intention whatsoever of
doing so.

There is a good deal of talk these days about the "conservative crack-up," and much of it is justified. But what
has cracked up is not the popular radicalism of the right but
rather the phony "populism" of the conservative establishment, which has signed up with the other establishments that
run the country. Even from their watchtowers on the Washington Beltway, the barons of this establishment can smell
the smoke of rebellion drifting in from the prairie, and they
know they didn't start the fire, can't control it, and can't put

it out. It won't take any more secret meetings in New York to learn that whoever does control that fire will determine the real political agenda for the next decade.

[September, 1990]

Revolution from the Middle

Despite last summer's brassy pronouncements that the owl had sung her watchsong on the towers of Capitol Hill, the oligarchs of Congress bit the reins in their teeth, squeezed their saddles between their knees, and lashed their mounts full into the maelstrom of constituents disgusted with pay-raises, privileges, perversion, and pretension. Some 96 percent of the incumbents managed to ride out of the electoral cyclone of 1990 still tall in the stirrups, and only the most foppish fell off. But no one, least of all the oligarchs themselves, should think that their victory means that the storm is over. The high mysteries of public opinion research show that Americans are more distrustful of Congress than ever before, and only by exploiting every sinister trick known to political science were the congressmen able to wheedle and whine their way back to Washington. You can fool some of the people some of the time — and that's enough.

Most voters — and only about 35 percent even bothered to show up at the hustings — may imagine that their own representative is somehow magically exempt from the inexorable laws that govern the degeneration of moral tissue once it hits the toxic atmosphere of political power. Hence, in the delusion that only their congressperson is a rock of rectitude in an ocean of sinful vacillation, citizens often were happy to send him back to the salons of Georgetown and the obscure pleasures of the congressional gymnasium. Then again, maybe they just didn't want him back home at all and took the view that employing him in Washington is the modern equivalent of a request from an emperor of ancient Rome that a courtier inflict his presence on the eternal city no more and betake himself to Thither Bithynia.

Yet the Middle American Revolution is not so easily thwarted. Despite the victory of the oligarchy last year, the frustrations of the shrinking American middle class remain deep and obvious even to the victors, and within the next decade their trumpets will sound again. The success of David Duke's underdog candidacy in Louisiana, the victory of Sen. Jesse Helms in North Carolina, the defeat of a proposition for a holiday honoring Martin Luther King in Arizona, the renaming of "The Rev. Dr. Martin Luther King Jr. Boulevard" in Harrisburg, Pa., and the popularity of tax and term limitation measures in several states showed that in the dark corners of the land the wheels of revolution are beginning to churn and that the natural fear of economic and cultural dispossession is the oil that greases them.

But those wheels will never get out of the ditch if mainstream conservatives are in the driver's seat. Never in recent history has the now largely defunct "conservative movement" produced a serious national political leader or accomplished much of anything on the national political scene. The most electrifying leaders of the American right — Joe McCarthy, George Wallace, and Ronald Reagan — emerged into prominence not because of the Latinate magazines and recondite philosophizing of organized American conservatism but due to their own inate ability to capture and express the aspirations of a repressed political class. Moreover, while the Middle American Revolution in some respects harbors some sentiments that conservatives share, in others it is hostile or indifferent to much of what conservatives in the United States have represented.

Throughout American history, the mainstream of conservative thought, from the anti-Federalists through the Confederacy to the resistance against the New Deal and the Great Society, has centered on the defense of liberty: states' rights, individual freedom, social and private as opposed to governmental responsibility, local as opposed to centralized policies. This was the theme of South Carolina's Sen. Robert Young Hayne's reply to Daniel Webster, when the southerner articulated one of the classic refutations of the northern Federalist-Whig vision of a united nation expanding economically under federal supervision. This also, as Shelby Foote argues in his three-volume Civil War series, was the rationale of Jefferson Davis in his inaugural address, declaiming that "all we ask is to be let alone," and it was the basis of the defensive military strategy of the Confederacy, which ultimately led to its defeat.

This too has been the approach of American conservatism in the twentieth century, which, despite the various philosophical costumes in which it has garbed itself, has taken its stand with strict constitutionalism, laissez faire economics, traditional social morality, and the freedom of individuals to pursue happiness in their own way. The central project of twentieth century conservatism has been to resist the aggressive imperialism of the bureaucratic leviathan in Washington and its sisters in the bureaucratized corporate and union economy and cultural regime, all of which fused together in the New Deal and its later derivatives; and the core of the conservative resistance has been the preservation or restoration of republican liberty.

That project was a realistic one as long as self-interested individuals and autonomous social institutions could restrain or maneuver within and around the apparatus of power that anti-conservative forces were building. Conservatives could argue that they were trying to conserve an existing and traditional social and political order, and they could find considerable support from small businessmen, farmers, and independent professionals who shared their animosity to the leveling leviathan.

But the only means of resistance their republican ideology permitted them was to engage in formal political contests within the framework of the constitutional system. The most popular and common path of conservative resistance has thus been purely and narrowly political; conservatives sought merely to hold up or reverse the leviathan's march by winning elections to Congress and the White House and by weaving bureaucratic intrigues within the leviathan's entrails. Eventually many of them became so enamored of politics, policy-cooking, and political responses that they evolved into the "Big Government conservatives" of today, centered exclusively in Washington, where they carefully plan how to arrange the deck chairs they're going to build for the *S.S. Titanic*.

By dashing onto the political playing fields designed by the architects of leviathan, political conservatives had to play by their rivals' rules in their rivals' game, so it shouldn't be surprising that conservatives wound up with pretty much the same thoughts and values that the architects have and wanted them to have. In recent years, conservative political leaders have increasingly regurgitated the basic premises of the liberal ideology they claim to be opposing and have quietly ceased to resist the left on much of anything except means. The government ought to promote equality, but affirmative action just isn't the way to achieve it. Civil liberties are what we want too, and the only thing wrong with pornography and drugs is that they might hurt children under twelve. Fraternity is terrific, and global democratic capitalism, spreading human rights and democracy, and presidential supremacy in foreign affairs are the right instruments by which isolationism can be overcome and planetary cosmopolitanism made to triumph forever. The mega-state constructed by every president from Wilson to Reagan should now be used for "conservative" ends, and we are all liberals with a big L when it comes to civil rights. Some — not just paleo-conservative dinosaurs — have begun to notice that the contemporary right seems to have turned into an ideological Xerox of liberalism.

Moreover, the conservative ideal of republican liberty and of being left alone allowed even those Americans who were non-political the fantasy of escape. All they really had to do to get away from the leviathan, it seemed, was evade the major burdens of taxation, attend to their own business, send their children to private schools, move to the suburbs, join private clubs, and in general avoid having to think about, confront, or challenge the ever-groping tentacles that sought to entwine them.

Some concluded that there was no point in resisting anyway. Whittaker Chambers came to believe that, and he ended his life in intense and private religious withdrawal, prophesying the apocalypse and preparing to gather up the fingernails of saints in self-imposed exile from modernity. At another extreme, H.L. Mencken also came to think that resistance to the New Deal regime was futile, and he withdrew into a passive Nietzschean cynicism. "At the moment," he wrote in his diary on June 1, 1942, "with the Roosevelt crusade to save humanity in full blast, my ideas are so unpopular that it is impossible, as it was from 1915 to 1920, for me to print them." Nor did it become possible again in his lifetime.

But if conservative activism was corruptive, conservative escapism has proved to be no less ineffective. Leviathan is relentless. By its very nature, it is never defensive but always aggressive. The millenarian dogmas that animate it, the vested interests that it serves, and the emotional resentments from which it breeds impel it forever to trample out the vineyards wherever they are found. It reaches into suburbs and private schools with its tax codes, its safety regulations, and its teachers' unions. It overturns laws enacted by states and cities and lets judges and bureaucratic gremlins dictate what form of government you must live under. It wrecks your neighborhood, tells you who to hire in your business and who to accept in your clubs, and teaches your children all there is to know about sexual perversion before they're old enough to go door to door by themselves on Halloween. It funds perverse art with your tax money and makes you display it in public museums. It gives your job to minorities who are less qualified than you. It denies college admission to your children and accepts minorities less qualified than they are. It makes it virtually impossible for the police to catch or the courts to punish killers and rapists, and when it does catch them, usually by accident, it "rehabilitates" them and turns them loose again on you, your wives, your children. It renames your streets, your schools, and your city parks for characters you've never heard of or have always despised. It orders you how to decorate public buildings for Christmas. It tells you your heritage, your literature, your art, your holidays, your religion, your music, your beliefs, your country, and your very skin color are garbage and mere tricks by which you and your class and your race have tyrannized mankind. Now it's considering how to make you pay reparations for slavery.

Leviathan decides to spread democracy and human rights throughout the world and plans wars in which you and your sons (and daughters) will have to fight and die — but never win — for principles and peoples you've never heard of. It blathers about "collective security," "disarmament," the "international rule of law," "interdependence," "global democracy," and "the New World Order," all of which are simply global versions of the same therapeutic managerial welfare state it has constructed domestically. It takes your money to pay for food stamps, illegitimate children, comfortable prisons, brainwashing disguised as child care, AIDS treatment centers, suicide clinics, sex education, racial sensitivity courses, multiculturalism, drug therapy, "death counselling," and all the other pathologies and neuroticisms that social managers imagine are the Higher Civilization. It snatches away your economic, political, social, and cultural autonomy by conscripting you into mass labor forces in office and factory, mass political organizations, mass residential complexes, mass transit systems, and mass entertainment and information networks where your passive emotional and mental responses are uniformly programmed by recorded laughter, applause, and music, and it thus housetrains you into a docile pet of the servile state. Leviathan won't stop at the city limits and leave the suburbs alone. There's nowhere to run anymore, and now that the country is facing recession, you couldn't afford to run even if you could.

What this means is that the traditional American conservatve defensive strategy is no longer practicable and that those who want to defend themselves against leviathan must go on the offensive. They must seek not just to restrain power but to gain power for themselves.

This does not mean, as neo-conservatives, the New Right, and Big Government conservatives believe, that the goal should be the mere capture of the existing governmental apparatus through winning elections and getting jobs in the bureaucracy. Control of the formal, legal apparatus of political power will not yield social and cultural power, what the Italian Marxist Antonio Gramsci called "cultural hegemony." In 1980, conservative Republicans won control of the White House and the Senate and for six years accomplished virtually nothing substantial in arresting the growth of leviathan or reversing its course. The reason for their failure had to do partly with the personal weaknesses of many of those who won but also with their neglect of aspiring to the cultural dominance that is the effective prerequisite for effective political power. The most radical of the conservatives of the 1980s, the New Right, was either oblivious to or utterly incompetent to deal with culture, not just in the sense of the higher arts, but also in the sense of using social and cultural institutions at the lower levels of family, neighborhood, schools, colleges, local communities, clubs, and workplaces to build a Middle American counter-culture within the belly of the beast.

Having shattered the traditional American cultural and social order into disparate fragments bound together only by universal and impersonal managerial routines and techniques, the leviathan regime is now confronted by a creature of its own making, an increasingly alienated and radicalized Middle American proletariat that is beginning to glimpse the abyss of its own cultural, economic and political serfdom just over the precipice it is approaching. The proletariat is also beginning to evolve a collective consciousness that can overcome the divisive, individuating, and purely defensive response offered by traditional conservatism and to forge a new and unified core from which an alternative subculture and an authentic radicalism of the right can emerge.

The dynamic of the Middle American Revolution is captured at the end of Tom Wolfe's *Bonfire of the Vanities*, when the flabby yuppy protagonist Sherman McCoy has been stripped of his wealth, his status, his wife, his mistress, his children, his friends, his class, his privacy, and his freedom. At last dispossessed of every external garment of his social identity, he turns to fight. Explaining what happened to him, he draws an analogy with a house pet that's been turned into a vicious watchdog. "They don't alter that dog's personality with dog biscuits or pills," he says. "They chain it up, and they beat it, and they bait it, and they taunt it, and they beat it some more, until it turns and bares its fangs and is ready for the final fight every time it hears a sound. ... The dog doesn't cling to the notion that he's a fabulous house pet in some terrific dog show, the way the man does. The dog gets the idea. The dog knows when it's time to turn into an animal and fight."

Or, as another fighter once said, you have nothing to lose but your chains of slavery.

[March, 1991]

Spearhead of the Revolution

The presidential games of 1992 are well more than a year away, but would-be Republican gladiators are already measuring George Bush for a quick thrust in the belly. Their plans may be premature. Though the president came close to wrecking his party by breaking his promise against new taxes and may yet make a fool of himself and his country abroad, he is no more seriously wounded than Ronald Reagan was in 1982 at a corresponding low point in his own presidency. Nevertheless, whatever happens between now and the moment when the political swordplay begins, the games these days seem to produce little more than yawns from the bored and largely passive citizen spectators. Barely 50 percent of qualified voters bothered to cast ballots in 1988, and the illusion that it really matters who sits in the White House is gradually dissipating.

One reason for the indifference to which slicko is crowned as the nation's chief executive is that the *de jure* office of the American presidency has become about as effective an instrument of power as Roseanne Barr would be on a basketball court. Swollen far beyond its natural proportions by a century's steady diet of the political equivalent of double cheeseburgers and hot fudge sundaes, the presidency today no longer consists of the individual who sits in the Oval Office and spends most of his day in harmless ceremonial. Today the presidency in fact is composed of pretty much the same sort of invisible munchkins who manage the corporate economy and the labyrinthine caverns of the dominant culture.

It is they, and not the occupants of formal office or the legal owners of corporate stock, who determine how, when, and in what direction the obese apparatus of power and wealth will waddle. The man in the grey flannel White House today confines most of his labors to munching cookies with visiting dignitaries, supervising Cabinet coffee clatchs, making periodic forays into the wilderness beyond the White House gates to receive honorary doctorates, and threatening foreign tyrants with visitations of globalist brimstone if they don't forthwith release whatever Yanks have been foolish enough to wander into their precincts. There is no doubt that the chief executive still performs such meaningless rituals of state, but the irrelevance of the president to real power emerges clearly whenever word of an Important Decision leaks out.

A Cabinet secretary is fired, a Supreme Court justice nominated, a treaty concluded, a law proposed, or a war begun, and no one, from the humblest chimneysweep to the most plugged-in pundit in Georgetown, ever imagines that the president had anything to do with it. Maybe it was the White House chief of staff, the secretary of state, the chairman of the Joint Chiefs, the first lady, the president's pollsters, the president's astrologer, or one or another of the castrated intellectuals that decorate the White House court who actually had the idea and guided it through the paper-clip jungle to the president's desk. But nobody thinks that the president himself conceived the idea, planned the strategy, or performed the work that made the decision real.

Of course, that doesn't mean he escapes the blame if the act of statecraft blows up in his and the nation's face. One real function the president still retains is to serve as national scapegoat for the crimes, failures, weaknesses, and follies of the executive bureaucracy. The contemporary president of the

United States does not resemble an emperor of Rome in its last days so much as he does one of the "divine kings" that the anthropologist James George Frazer wrote about. Chosen by the local priesthood to reign for a year of splendor and indulgence in every known human appetite, the holy monarch would eventually be pitched into a volcano or have his entrails ripped out to divert the wrath of whatever vengeful gods the Third World of antiquity adored. But of course, during his year of opulence, there was never any question of letting his divine majesty actually run things. His only function was to vegetate in sacerdotal luxury until the dread day of atonement fell.

The engorgement of the American presidency by the managerial priesthood of the executive branch means that it has ceased to make much practical difference which individual or party holds the office. A new president may bring new lapdogs to court and his wife may order new wallpaper for the White House bathrooms, but the real rulers, invisible and immoveable, never even flutter their eyelids when the body politic twitches in the quadrennial presidential election.

It follows that conservatives, who have dreamed and drooled at the prospect of placing one of their own in the Oval Office ever since Herbert Hoover was defenestrated, ought to find better things to do with themselves. In 1980 they actually thought their millennium had arrived, and indeed Mr. Reagan was about as reasonable a facsimile of the conservative ideal as the political chemistry of the late twentieth century could brew. But, while Mr. Reagan occasionally voiced inspiring sentiments, made a few good appointments, and even presided over an at least temporary economic recovery, not even the Gipper succeeded in staying the course of governmental enlargement. When he left office, the Department of Education was even bigger than when he entered, despite his promise to abolish both it and the Energy Department, and he even added an entirely new appendage in the form of the Department of Veterans Affairs to the already bloated federal trunk.

Yet the presidency throughout American history has always served as the spearhead by which a new elite has broken through the intermediary institutions in which an old elite is lodged. In the First Republic of the early nineteenth century, the main social conflict was between, on the one hand, northern commercial and industrial interests that sought to use the federal government to help fill their own pockets and "develop" the rest of the country and, on the other, southern agrarian interests, which, to be sure, made use of Washington to protect slavery as much as possible through the Constitution and the Fugitive Slave Law but in general had every reason to keep centralized power as limited as possible. Once the representatives of the southern interests had seceded in 1861, their rivals in the north saw their opportunity and grabbed it.

Lincoln's presidency (and perhaps Secretary of War Edwin Stanton as much as the president himself) served as the icepick that broke through the crystallized institutions of the First Republic and allowed the waters of an emerging bourgeois elite to flow toward political, economic, and cultural control. Once the bourgeoisie had won, it had little use for an expanded presidency, and it ruled largely through its own intermediary institutions in Congress, the local jurisdictions that controlled Congress, and the informal, decentralized, and private apparatus that the elite constructed in small towns, private corporations, and state and local governments across the country.

The corruption and incompetence that ensued from bourgeois dominance is known to every schoolboy, though somehow the connection between the excesses of the Gilded Age and the crushing of the South is never noticed. In any case, by the early twentieth century, a new elite of rising technocratic and managerial forces was challenging the bourgeois order and making use of Progressivist ideology to discredit bourgeois institutions.

Of course, they saw in the presidency a convenient instrument by which they could centralize power and undermine the hegemony of their bourgeois rivals. Progressivist ideologues like *The New Republic*'s Herbert Croly looked on the Lincoln presidency as a model for their own revolution, and with the two Roosevelts and Woodrow Wilson they succeeded in entrenching themselves in the vast regulatory woodwork of the executive branch that they built. A half century later the dominant managerial class is still there and is still dependent on the imperial presidency, and, like the bourgeois elite that it displaced, has also become corrupt, self-serving, incompetent, and oligarchic.

For a brief moment in the 1970's it looked as though their power was being effectively challenged by yet another rising social force of Middle Americans, and both Richard Nixon's "New American Majority" and the "New Right" of the later part of the decade seemed about to oust the incumbent managerial elite. In the first half of the Reagan presidency, however, it became clear that it wouldn't happen. It couldn't happen then, for two reasons.

First, Mr. Reagan and his supporters never developed an alternative base of cultural power by which they could legitimize their efforts. They did not do so mainly because they never understood clearly what they represented — not a clean-up squad sent in to mop up the mess left by Jimmy Carter but a new set of engineers and architects who were supposed to tear down the old structure and build anew. Hence, Mr. Reagan and most of his advisers, wordsmiths, and satellites continued to justify their policies in terms acceptable to the dominant culture and the interests it serves. Mr. Reagan continually invoked Franklin Roosevelt and the New Deal, and the supply-side proselytizers and resident anti-communists were always summoning from the vasty deep the spirits of John F. Kennedy, Hubert Humphrey, and Henry Jackson, while everyone rushed to prostrate himself before the chief deity of the liberal pantheon, the Divine Doctor himself, Martin Luther King, Jr. The Reagan administration presented itself simply as a corrective to liberal errors in navigation, not as a new ship charting a new course. In the end, the Middle American Radicalism to which Mr. Reagan had appealed in his early political career and in his 1980 campaign proved to be too immature, too poorly understood by the Gipperites, and too lacking in an independent cultural and political consciousness to serve as the chart by which the new course could be planned.

Secondly, any effort to raise Middle American consciousness for a new cultural identity and a power base resting on it was thwarted by the manipulative genius of the incumbent elite. By inserting cultural managers like William Bennett in the National Endowment for the Humanities and the Education Department, by placing corporate mandarins like Donald Regan and George Shultz in charge of economic and foreign policy, by letting George Bush and his friends wield more influence than they had a right to, and by relying on such silver-throated men of the people as Howard Baker and Robert Dole to run the Senate for him, Mr. Reagan ensured that nothing he did would ever seriously threaten the foundations of the ruling groups he had campaigned against. His chosen lieutenants and the bureaucratic morlocks who labored beneath the surface of visible politics simply aborted any inclinations to radical action that might have stirred in the administration's womb.

The emasculation of the Reagan presidency before it ever reached political puberty was, in retrospect, predictable. The underlying radical impulses of Reaganism were simply too embryonic to be able to take and exercise power. Nor, for all the disenchantment with George Bush and his court, have they grown up very much since Mr. Reagan departed.

In effect, what this means is that genuinely radical conservative forces cannot expect to accomplish much simply by winning the White House. Political power in the absence of an alternative social and cultural power base will inevitably be swallowed by the forces that remain dominant in society and culture and which are particularly dense in the presidency, the institutional heart of the regime. If the Right really wants to win power, it will have to create that kind of counter-culture before it can expect to gain much from electoral gladhanding and horse-trading. Once it does so and is willing to mobilize its counter-cultural base against the incumbent elite and its institutional loci of power, it will find the presidency the natural instrument for a new Middle American revolution.

[April, 1991]

After the Republic

J ust because it looks like a Republic and quacks like a
Republic doesn't mean it's really a Republic. In ancient
Rome, after Julius and Augustus Caesar got through with
the civil wars, proscriptions, and purges that spelled the death
of the old Roman nobility, the state still looked and quacked
like the republic it had been in the days of Cincinnatus and
Cato the Elder. There were still consuls and vestal virgins and
all the other trappings of the old republican constitution. There
were still law courts and elections. There was still the shell of
the old pagan religion of the sons of Romulus.

But everyone knew it wasn't so, that a century of demagogues and dictators had ruptured the republican duck, that the
Caesars had finally polished off the reality of republican government and set up their own sweet little autocracy. "Despotism, enthroned at Rome," wrote historian Ronald Syme in *The
Roman Revolution*, "was arrayed in robes torn from the corpse
of the Republic."

So it is today in the United States. The Constitution still exists
and remains a standing topic of Fourth of July oratory. We still
have elections and even the vestiges of that aristocratic balance
wheel, the electoral college. We still have republican (but, even
today, not really democratic) representation in the Senate.

But despite the persistence of these republican forms,
the reality is quite different — a mass democracy in which

elected officials are more and more irrelevant and corrupt as their powers and duties are usurped by bureaucratic elites that cannot be removed. Despotism, masked in republican costume, is not yet enthroned, but already it whispers sweetly in the ears of those who sit in the consular chairs of the leviathan state.

Why did the American Republic die, and why can't it be restored? The generation of Americans at the time the Constitution was written was immersed in republican thought and principles, and the Framers consistently tried to establish a republic that could avoid the anarchy, demagoguery, and tyranny to which most previous republics — in Greece, Rome, Renaissance Italy, Holland, and England — had succumbed. But, if the republic they established is in fact moribund, either they made a mistake or else something has happened in the last 200 years that they never anticipated.

Writing on the different schools of republican thought that permeated the United States in its infancy, historian Forrest McDonald notes that virtually all of them shared a common set of beliefs. "The vital — that is life-giving — principle of republics was public virtue," a term that rang rather differently from its resonance in modern ears.

> Not coincidentally, public, like virtue, derives from Latin roots signifying manhood: "the public" included only independent adult males. Public virtue entailed firmness, courage, endurance, industry, frugal living, strength, and above all, unremitting devotion to the weal of the public's corporate self, the community of virtuous men. It was at once individualistic and communal: individualistic in that no member of the public could be dependent upon any other and still be reckoned a member of the public; communal in that every man gave himself totally to the good of the public as a whole. If public virtue declined, the republic declined, and if it declined too far, the republic died.

Americans were divided on the question of exactly how public virtue could be preserved and institutionalized, but Southern republicans in particular tended to insist on its concrete social and economic roots rather than, as New England Puritan republicanism did, on its purely moral and religious supports. In the "agrarian republicanism" of the South, writes Professor McDonald, "virtue, independence, liberty, and the ownership of unencumbered real property were inextricably bound together. ... ownership of land begat independence, independence begat virtue, and virtue begat republican liberty."

There was, in short, what historian J.G.A. Pocock calls a "sociology of liberty": liberty was not merely something that could flourish in a vacuum because everyone wanted it; it blossomed only when and if the citizens were socially independent — if they owned their own property, ruled their own families, ran their own farms and businesses, bore their own arms in their own defense, took responsibility for their own failures and mistakes, and earned and enjoyed their own rewards, then and only then could men govern their own selves, as individuals or as a people, as a republic.

The fierce attachment to the ideal of independence in classical republican thought is the reason republicans didn't (and don't) much like what is today called "Big Government" or its brother, Big Business. Bigness means dependency. In the eighteenth century, bigness meant the swollen dynastic states of Europe, with their courtiers and pensioners begging their livings from the monarchs and their mistresses. It meant entrenched aristocracies, established churches, protected guilds, privileged monopolies, entailed estates, absentee landlords, enclosed lands that once belonged to independent yeomen, and crazy, crooked, dirty cities where dispossessed yeomen herded together to form mobs that ran amok whenever their masters failed to feed them on time.

It was not Europe's lack of "opportunity" and social mobility or the mere fact of inequality that disgusted most republicans so much as it was the swallowing of independent men and institutions by the dynastic leviathans of the age. There couldn't be a republic in eighteenth-century Europe because its rulers as well as its ruled were not independent and had long since been smothered by the corruption, sycophancy, and slavery that dependence breeds.

It can be argued (and it may well be true) that at least some of the Framers were not enchanted by the prospect of old-fashioned republican virtue and its rather muscular vision of social independence, that Hamilton and Madison in particular entertained visions of a more grandiose state that would elevate the nation in wealth and power, and that they essentially redefined republicanism so as to accommodate their ideas and ambitions.

Indeed, it was so argued by the anti-Federalists and their successors, and for the first 70 years of the young republic's life, the scale and purposes of the national government were the principal issues of political debate in the controversies over the Tariff, the National Bank, "internal improvements," and slavery. The debate came to an end in the Civil War, when the advocates of a national state dedicated to filling the pockets of the citizens triumphed in the tread of the legions of the gentle Abraham.

Be that as it may, by the end of the nineteenth century, the American Republic remained intact, as did the social independence and public virtue on which it rested. Prior to World War I, writes Robert Nisbet, the main contact most Americans had with the federal government was at the Post Office, and until the bonds of industrial and technological conglomeration were forged, Americans — or at least the middle-class core of American civilization — retained the social, economic, cultural, and political independence that made a republic possible.

Today this is not the case. Twentieth-century technology and organization — in Big Government, Big Business, and Big Culture — have increased far beyond the compact scale on which republican independence is possible and much farther than even the dynastic states of the *ancien régime* could comprehend. The American middle class today is dependent on corporations, unions, universities, and the national state itself for its income, and it is income — not an ethic or culture such as the nineteenth century bourgeois middle class possessed — that defines the contemporary middle class.

The mega-state and its tentacles touch and twist at every joint of our lives, and their operations are directed by permanent and largely invisible bureaucratic and managerial elites, not primarily by officeholders or independent property owners. Those who hold office spend much of their time trying to shovel federal fodder into their constituents' troughs. Mass media and mass cultural organizations in education and religion bind virtually all Americans into the same vast audience, poked and prodded by the same images, ideas, information, and misinformation to emit the same mental and emotional responses.

At the end of the twentieth century, Americans have been absorbed within and become dependent on massive organizations and technologies that are far too large, too complex, and too distant for most of us to control or even to influence. Under that kind of dependency, the social and moral disciplines that make personal and republican self-government possible wither away.

Hence, the rise of mass organizations and the elites that run them and our own dependence on them have paralleled the explosion of social breakdowns — crime, suicides, drug use, sexual excess and deviation, the brutalization of women and children, the collapse of families and communities, the pursuit of hedonism and immediate gratification, the glorification of the sick, the weak, and the weird. Mass society breeds dependency; dependency breeds corruption; and corruption breeds slavery. When independence and public virtue decline too far, the republic dies, even though despots may robe themselves in its garments.

Once the sociology of liberty is destroyed, it cannot be restored. Once the institutions and habits of independent discipline have withered, they do not naturally blossom again. Most Americans today are content with the mega-state, the cult of consumption that a bureaucratized economy encourages, and the titillations, fantasies, and diversions of the mass media. The only discontent most of us have with the mega-state is when we have to pay for somebody else to get more from it — in welfare, services, subsidies, tax breaks — than we get.

Democratic politics in the leviathan state is never about dismantling or reducing leviathan but always about forcing somebody else to pay for what we want from it. A mass democracy of interest groups, lobbies, ideological movements, and opinion clusters replaces the "unremitting devotion to the weal of the public's corporate self" that animated classical republicans, and the engorgement of leviathan is accelerated by the twin engines of a bureaucratic elite intent on enlarging its own power and the mass voting blocs it feeds, just as eighteenth-century demagogues fed their mobs. Unlike a republic, mass democracy doesn't restrain power; democracy unleashes power.

Except for a few right-wing eggheads, no one seriously contemplates restoring the republic; no one seriously wants to because no one has any material interest in it. Hence, the republic will not be restored.

Those few who remain attached to republicanism thus find themselves in the position of republican theorists like the Roman historian Tacitus and Niccolò Machiavelli, both of whom had seen their republics gurgle down the drainpipes of history. Both of them understood that republican liberty is not something you get by just wishing for it or believing in it, that in the absence of the public virtue on which republicanism is grounded, you cannot have liberty.

Tacitus had the good fortune to live in an age when the incumbent Caesars were not stark-raving lunatics but relatively benevolent despots, so he didn't need to worry too much about the more unpleasant aspects of gilded slavery. Machiavelli, who was imprisoned and tortured by the gangsters who took over Florence after the fall of its republic, perhaps worried more, and he had a more immediate grasp of what happens when a republic is corrupt and dying.

At that point, he wrote, "it becomes necessary to resort to extraordinary measures, such as violence and arms, and above all things to make one's self the absolute master of the state, so as to be able to dispose of it at will." Machiavelli understood that this kind of authoritarian rule was not a real solution or a restoration of liberty but simply the natural consequence of corruption; "for men whose turbulence could not be controlled by the simple force of law can be controlled in a measure only by an almost regal power."

The consolidation of political, economic, and cultural power on just such a regal scale has in fact largely occurred in the United States already. The question that the dying Republic yields, therefore, is not whether the Republic will be restored but rather how those Middle Americans who were the nucleus of the American Republic, who retain the vestiges of public virtue, and who now find themselves the victims of the new imperium can displace the elite that now prevails. The issue, in other words, is: Who, in the wrecked vessel of the American Republic, is to be master?

[August, 1991]

State and Revolution

If the American Republic is defunct, and if most Americans no longer subscribe to the classical republicanism that defined the Republic as its public orthodoxy, what is the principal issue of American politics? Ever since the Progressive Era, the issue that has divided Americans into the two political and ideological camps of "Right" and "Left" has been whether or not to preserve the Republic. The Progressives (at least their dominant wing) argued that the small-scale government, entrepreneurial business economy, and localized and private social and cultural fabric that made a republic possible was obsolete at best and at worst repressive and exploitative. They and their descendants in New Deal/Great Society liberalism pushed for an enlarged state fused with corporations and unions in the economy and with massive, bureaucratized cultural and educational organizations. In contrast, the "Right" pulled in the opposite direction, defending the Republic and the social and economic structure that enabled republicanism to flourish, but with less and less success and with ever-diminishing understanding of what they were doing.

Today the conflict over that issue is finished. The Progressivist empire has replaced the old American Republic, and even on the self-proclaimed "Right" today, virtually no one other than the beleaguered "paleo-conservatives" defends republicanism in anything like its pristine form. The collapse of the conflict over republicanism is the main reason why the labels "Left" and "Right" no longer make much sense and also why — much more than the end of the Reagan administration and the Cold War — the "conservative coalition" of the Reagan era is falling apart. Mr. Reagan's main legacy was to show his followers, who for decades groused and griped against "Big Government," that they too could climb aboard the Big Government hay ride and nibble crumbs at its picnic. With such "conservatism" now centered mainly in Washington and its exponents happily dependent on the federal mega-state, the historic *raison d'etre* of the American "Right" has ceased to exist. Such conservatives no longer even pretend to want to preserve or restore the old Republic, and it now turns out that even when they said they did, it was all pretty much a charade anyway.

Nevertheless, the end of the conflict over the Republic and of the battle between Left and Right does not mean that there are no conflicts at all. Indeed, the American imperium, having few roots in the population except in so far as it can feed its client constituencies, is riven by conflicts. The empire might be able to strike back, but it has never been able to formulate its own orthodoxy that would distinguish it from traditional republicanism. That indeed is why the mega-state has retained the forms of republicanism. Unable to legitimize itself through the ideology of Progressivist liberalism, it steals the clothes of its republican predecessor to justify its revolutionary agenda.

At the heart of the empire — or mega-state, or managerial regime, or leviathan, or whatever you want to call it — there is a vacuum, and the main issue of the last decade of this century and the first decade of the next will be over what is going to fill that empty space. The ability to fill it, to articulate a public orthodoxy for the country, is in large part what it means to be master of the imperium, for whoever is able to acquire enough cultural power to define what the mega-state is supposed to do and for whom it is supposed to do it will achieve Antonio

Gramsci's "cultural hegemony" and will carve his own initials on the blank slate of the empire.

One of the principal contestants for hegemony in the mega-state will be the largely Middle American constituency of the now-decapitated American Right. The end of the Left-Right conflict and the absorption of its leadership within the mega-state means that the mass following of the Right has become a body without a head. That following thus finds itself, its interests and values, unrepresented in the contest for control of the mega-state of the next century, and that situation cannot last. Sooner or later, if Middle Americans are not to become extinct, they will generate a new, independent social and political identity or consciousness and will construct a movement based on that consciousness that will demand not only representation in, but also dominance of, the regime.

But they will not, as their forebears did, demand republicanism. Middle Americans are a diverse bunch, consisting of small businessmen in the manufacturing sector of the economy, small farmers burdened with debt and confronted with absorption by conglomerate agribusiness, and white ethnic blue-collar workers who find their jobs disappearing because of foreign competition and their advancement thwarted by mega-state-mandated racial and gender quotas. What these and similar groups share, despite their diversity, is a common frustration with the mega-state as it is presently structured, along with a seemingly paradoxical dependence on it.

Their frustrations might lead them toward a revival of classical republican, small-government conservatism, but their dependence on the state forbids it. Middle Americans are as much wrapped up in the tentacles of the mega-state as the elite that runs it or the underclass that is its main beneficiary. Middle Americans buy their homes with loans provided by the federal government. They educate their children in public schools and send them to colleges, themselves recipients of federal funds, with federal student aid. They work for corporations regulated by and linked to the state and are members of labor unions protected by federal laws. They receive federal farm subsidies, and the food they produce and eat, the highways on which they travel, the air they breathe, and the television they watch all are subject to the laws and regulations of the federal mega-state. Most Americans, Middle or not, lodge few objections to this kind of regimentation; what they do object to is that it doesn't work all that well — that is, that they don't get from it as much as they want or expect — or that federal regimentation often seems to help others more than it helps them. Middle Americans don't object to the mega-state in principle, but they do object to it in practice.

Hence, the agenda of an authentic Middle American political consciousness would include retaining many of the structures and functions of the mega-state, and in this respect it would not be attractive to most paleo-conservatives or paleo-libertarians. Middle Americans would insist on a state that protected their material security — through such "middle-class welfare" programs as health insurance, unemployment benefits, pensions, and labor regulations, as well as economic policies intended to secure their jobs, farms, and businesses.

Yet, at the same time, a Middle American agenda would involve a fairly radical dismantlement and restructuring of the mega-state. As it is presently constituted, the mega-state exists for the purpose of social manipulation. Its elite, trained in the techniques of social engineering and social therapy, gains power and budgetary resources by inventing social "problems" and "crises" and then designing and applying "solutions" for them. Obviously, every "solution" creates yet another "problem," so the mission of the bureaucratic elite (and its cousins in universities and think-tanks) is never complete. The solutions are

characteristically egalitarian and redistributive and assist the
elite in delegitimizing, reconstructing, and otherwise manipulating traditional Middle American institutions and beliefs.

Moreover, most of the "problems" the elite invents are
always located within or about the underclass — racism, poverty, crime, cities, AIDS, drugs, illiteracy, illegitimacy and
family breakdown, infant mortality, the lack of underclass political representation, etc., etc. — so that a vast amount of money,
energy, and attention is devoted to the underclass, not to Middle
Americans, who nevertheless are expected to pay for the
underclass as well as for the elite and the programs that support
it. The mega-state, then, as it is presently structured, is an
apparatus that largely serves the interests of the elite and its
underclass ally, at the expense, material and cultural, of the
middle class.

A serious Middle American political consciousness would
therefore reject and seek to excise the problem-solution ratchet
that is the motor of the present regime as well as other functions intended to manipulate and deconstruct traditional institutions. Thus, the preoccupation of the incumbent elite with racism, sexism, "civil rights," social "pathologies" that are little
more than normative Middle American institutions and beliefs,
and the whole apparatus in state and culture by which white,
male "hegemony" is challenged and undermined would have
to go. This would involve more than simply formulating new
policies and punching a few buttons on the mega-state's control
panel. It would involve ripping the entrails out of the elite
itself by eliminating much of the bureaucracy and its agencies
and decoupling the elite of the mega-state from its Siamese
twins in the cultural organs. Abolishing tax-exemptions, subsidies, and federal contracts for the universities and foundations where manipulative social policy is born would be a practical way to begin.

It is the radicalism of such a Middle American consciousness that definitively separates it from both New Deal/Great Society liberalism and from the "Big Government conservatism" and neo-conservatism that flourish today. The real goal of the liberal mega-state was not to secure the well-being of Middle Americans but to level and destroy their distinctive cultural identity by identifying it as the "social environment" that bred pathologies and dysfunctions. The real goal of "Big Government conservatives" and neo-conservatives has never been to dismantle the structures of the mega-state and redesign its functions but simply to capture them and make them work more efficiently, with "efficiency" implicitly defined as the more practical realization of their liberal goals. "Big Government conservatives" do nothing to challenge the orientation of the mega-state toward the interests of the elite and its tame underclass, and their whole agenda seems to be centered on locking that orientation into place.

Middle Americans have long piggy-backed on mainstream conservatism, but they have done so only by obscuring (or failing to understand completely) the differences that distinguish their interests and aspirations from the increasingly rootless and fruitless fixations of the conventional Right. With the collapse of the Right and the obsolescence (not to say the fraudulence) of its republican ideology, Middle Americans have an opportunity — and, indeed, face the necessity — of articulating a consciousness that more accurately reflects their material interests and their cultural identity.

For those who still adhere to classical republicanism, the emergence of a Middle American radicalism would no doubt be distasteful, but their own long lack of success in reviving their political ideals ought perhaps to induce a certain humility among them, as well as a willingness to postpone displays of ideological passion in order to consummate later an eventual and more enduring fulfillment. If the classical republican ideal is ever to rise from its ashes, it can do so only among those who retain even now the vestigial moral and social disciplines that render republican government possible. The only remaining locus of such republican disciplines in the United States at the end of the twentieth century is the Middle American stratum that is now a hammer without a head. If it can construct its own head, it may be able to forge a new civil order from which a republican phoenix can someday be reborn.

[September, 1991]

The 'New Class of the Downtrodden'

Back in the days when Southern merchants had to take the Ku Klux Klan seriously, the knights of the Invisible Empire liked to play a neat little trick on a storeowner who had strayed too far from the path of racial rectitude the secret society demanded of him. Several Klansmen in plain clothes would drop by the store and leave calling cards among the items of merchandise on display. When the merchant or his clerks found the cards later, they would read, on one side, the polite inscription, "You have just been visited by the Knights of the Ku Klux Klan." Turning it over, they would see another, more ominous message: "How would you like another visit?"

In October, 1990, fresh from winning 60 percent of the white vote in Louisiana's senatorial election and forcing the Republican candidate to withdraw, former Klansman David Duke called on the U.S. Senate. The occasion was the Senate's effort to override President Bush's veto of the so-called "Civil Rights Bill of 1990." Brooding silently in the gallery above the Senate floor, Mr. Duke didn't leave any cards, burn any crosses, or lynch any lawmakers, but the senators below nevertheless understood the message. By one vote they failed to override the veto, and the Civil Rights Bill died. They didn't want another visit.

But that was less than a month before one of those nasty little inconveniences of American government known as congressional elections, and even without Mr. Duke's presence in the gallery, it's unlikely the senators would have proceeded to pass the bill over the veto. In November, Sen. Jesse Helms won re-election after deploying on television a savage advertisement attacking his black opponent's support of affirmative action, quotas, minority set-asides, and the Civil Rights Bill itself, and in California Pete Wilson won the governorship by making similar noises about white racial discontent. For all its flaws, nothing concentrates the mind of a sitting politician so wonderfully as an approaching election.

By January, 1991, however, the crisis was over. There would be no election for another two whole years, and so literally the first thing the new Congress did was to re-introduce the same bill. Last spring, the House again passed it, and Mr. Bush, who never fails to mention the bill without swearing that he really wants to pass some kind of civil rights measure but just not this one, again threatens to veto it.

The House passed the bill by exactly the same margin as last year and therefore failed to cough up sufficient votes to override yet another veto. For opponents of the measure, that might seem to be good news, but in the absence of an impending election, celebration is unwarranted. No matter how concentrated their minds were in the fall of 1990, politicians characteristically suffer from short attention spans, and it may require some further mental concentration on their part for them to remember who it is they really work for.

Nor, perhaps, can we rely on Mr. Bush to cast his veto as he did before. Even as he slew the civil rights beast in its legislative cave in 1990, he was preparing to violate his most vocal pledge against raising taxes, and his blood-oaths of another veto can be taken no more seriously than his now notorious line in 1988 about "read my lips." Mr. Bush may do a mean Clint Eastwood when he's dealing with Saddam Hussein, but when it comes to domestic affairs, he's Alan Alda.

Moreover, the pressures on the president from the bowels of his own party and its allies are such that he may wobble. Earlier this year, the Business Roundtable, a gaggle of Big Business managers ever ready to do deals with the hard left, sought to make friendly with the civil rights elite to push the main features of the Democratic bill through. The bill's close regulation of hiring and promotion practices within private business firms would create burdens mainly on small, Middle American enterprises, and the commodores of high capitalism have ever been prepared to pitch their smaller brethren over the topsides. As the *Congressional Quarterly* pointed out in trying to explain why Big Business favored a civil rights bill that would place legal and political restrictions on its own employment practices, "companies such as AT&T and American Express could gain the good will of working with civil rights groups and the opportunity to address their interests in the bill. Public relations is important to consumer-driven businesses such as AT&T, which in 1989 was threatened with a boycott during labor talks."

Big Business, furthermore, is also getting dressed for the day when whites will be a minority in the United States, and, unlike some people, its hard-eyed managers know very well that the racial and demographic revolution is going to change some things. William Coleman, who was President Ford's transportation secretary and is now chairman of the NAACP's Legal Defense and Educational Fund, is pretty explicit about this. "A chief executive officer of a major corporation today has to realize that by the year 2000 more than half of his work force will be women and/or minorities," he says. "It's in their best interest to get the best qualified people."

The eagerness of corporate magnates to clink their glasses with the civil rights elite, even at the expense of small business, the qualifications of white male workers, and the freedom of their own firms, was matched by the defection from Mr. Bush's ranks of Missouri's Republican Sen. John Danforth and a flying squad of liberated Republicans last summer. Mr. Danforth, after the House failed to muster enough votes to override a veto of the Democrats' civil rights bill this year, sponsored his own bill in opposition to both the president's and the Democrats'. If Mr. Bush doesn't buy the terms of the Danforth measure, the Missouri Republican and his band of stalwarts could help override his veto in the Senate.

And, finally, Mr. Bush's own bill is not all that different in basic concept from what the Democrats are pushing. The major objection to the Democratic measure is that it would require employers to prove that they're not discriminating in hiring practices on the basis of race and sex. It reverses five Supreme Court decisions that relieved employers of that burden. (It's amazing, after all the whining during the Warren and Burger eras that the Court's rulings were the voice of God, how quickly Congress can gut the court's decisions if they transgress the divine revelations of the civil rights scriptures.) Though Democrats make much of the absence of the word "quota" in their legislation, Mr. Bush is no doubt correct when he argues that their bill's requirement that employers would have to prove they're not discriminating means in effect that businesses would have to establish racial and gender quotas.

But, as liberal pundit Michael Kinsley rather gleefully points out, Mr. Bush's own bill does pretty much the same thing. While the Democrats' measure demands that employers prove that hiring standards have "significant and manifest relationship to ... job performance," Mr. Bush's bill would require them to prove that a hiring practice "serves in a significant way ... legitimate employment goals." The opacity of such weasel-words as "manifest" and "significant" is such that whole armies of bureaucrats, lawyers, and judges can make sport with them for decades, and both liberal Democrats and conservative Republicans nowadays don't even blink at passing federal legislation that prescribes what "goals" employers must have, whether their "goals" are "legitimate" or not, and how the "legitimate goals" must be legally fulfilled.

The whole upshot is the very unpleasant truth that Republicans and mainstream conservatives are no more reliable than the hard left when it comes to resisting the perpetual revolution that "civil rights" involves. Wedded to an ideology that espouses "equality of opportunity" as the sole legitimizing principle of the "American experiment" and to the system of produce-and-consume capitalism that the egalitarian slogan is supposed to justify, Republicans care for property rights and limited government only in so far as they can be persuaded that these are effective instruments of the *summum bonum* of economic growth and mass affluence. Married to corporate and political interests that are themselves dependent on immigrants and minorities as workers, consumers, and voters, the Republican Party and mainstream conservatives are unable to resist the demographic, racial, political, and cultural revolution these interests and their underclass allies drive.

But many Middle Americans who have long since tumbled to the Democrats' prostration to special interests and elites seem to remain blind to the same phenomenon among Republicans. Last June, just before the House passed the Democrats' bill, the *Washington Post* interviewed white ethnic workers in southwest Chicago, the location of "trim 1950s style neighborhoods that are home to thousands of city workers and utility company employees." The debate about the civil rights bill there, reported the *Post*, concerns "more than a political struggle" between Democrats and Republicans. "It's about who gets hired and who gets promoted, who gets ahead enough to send his kids to college and who gets left behind."

The Democrats, city firefighter Mike Callaghan told the *Post*, are "creating a new class of the downtrodden, and that's us. The guys they are stepping on are middle-class white Americans, and we are leaving in droves to vote for the Republican Party." Faced with the disintegration of their culture and their way of life, citizens like Mr. Callaghan now encounter the last, logical turn of the leviathan state's meatgrinder in the politically engineered destruction of their jobs and careers and the material security the leviathan has always claimed to guarantee them.

But Mr. Callaghan ought to be advised that George Bush, the Business Roundtable, Sen. Danforth, and the other chiefs in the Republican wigwam aren't very different from their Democratic rivals and that simply changing parties won't save Middle American scalps. Mr. Bush, of course, will make sure that Mr. Callaghan knows all about Willie Horton and the Pledge of Allegiance and will wave plenty of yellow ribbons to stir authentic Middle American patriotic juices. But after the president wins his vote, his mind will wander off to the New World Order, a thousand points of light, and other luminescent cow droppings that do nothing to protect the core of American civilization from its coming cultural and economic dispossession. If the "new class of the downtrodden" in America's suburbs and farms wants to save itself from that destruction, it will have to do more than vote Republican. One visit, it turns out, wasn't quite enough. How would Washington like to have another?

[November, 1991]

America First

No slogan is more conducive to an outbreak of pimples on the cheeks of the establishment than the phrase "America First," and if it contained no other merit or meaning, that alone might constitute sufficient reason to emblazon it on your bumper stickers. Yet, in the last decade of the twentieth century, as One-Worlders, New Worlders, and Pax Americanoes proudly plot how the United States and its distinctive peoples and culture shall evaporate, "America First" is more than an irritant. It is the central concept of a new nationalism that prescribes not only a new foreign policy that reflects the interests of the United States but also a vision and an understanding of what America is and what it should be.

For most of the fifty years since the attack on Pearl Harbor, the idea of defining and pursuing an American interest apart from the common interests of U.S. allies in the Cold War was not practicable. Facing a common threat to their interests and existence in the form of Soviet Communism, the United States and its partners in Western Europe, Latin America, Asia, Africa, and the Middle East had every reason to subordinate their particular and immediate national interests to the paramount goal of resisting the threat. Granted the reality of the Communist menace — through military conquest, nuclear extortion, subversion, and the manipulation of surrogates and satellites — and granted also that a strategy of "liberation" or "rollback" would not be adopted, the general way in which the

"West" (a nearly meaningless term that today includes Japan, Taiwan, and South Korea as well as other non-Western states) responded to Soviet Communism through a policy of "containment" made sense.

But containment as it developed involved not only surrounding the Soviet Union with a periphery of regional security pacts but also building an embryonic world government in the form of the United Nations, the World Court, the IMF and World Bank, entire volumes of "treaty regimes" and executive agreements (some of which remain secret), and the vast labyrinth of the national security bureaucracy joined to a foreign policy establishment in universities, foundations, corporations, banks, law firms, and Congress. Long before Soviet Communism began to turn belly up, this whole complex had become a self-sustaining and self-interested elite, closely linked to and part of the larger managerial elite that has come to prevail in American and European governments, economies, and cultures.

If there were some purpose to the existence and functions of this elite during the Cold War, today, with the demise of Soviet Communism and the withering of its satellites, there is very little. Nevertheless, like any elite, the one that presided over the Cold War is unwilling to renounce its power and position, and for some years it has been busily inventing new rationales for itself. The creation of "global democracy" and the management of the "global economy" and the "global environment" are two of the most common such formulas, though periodically the apologists for globalism also invent new "threats" of one kind or another to which we must dedicate ourselves to resisting and fighting.

Yet all of these new globalist ideologies ring hollow, and none has so far offered any compelling reasons why Americans should continue to spend their time, their money, or their lives solving the problems of other peoples, paying for their errors, or fighting their wars. Moreover, there is good reason why Americans should resist the new formulas and the agendas and interests they rationalize.

The globalist agenda includes not only continued U.S. intervention in and management of foreign events but also the diminution or abolition of the United States itself as a sovereign nation, an autonomous economy, and a distinctive culture. Hence, globalists support and promote the subordination of U.S. national interests and sovereign freedom of action to transnational organizations and their bureaucratic elites that supposedly represent a "global community" or "global economy." They also advance the amalgamation of the nation and its people and civilization into a globally homogeneous "mankind" through toleration of massive immigration, imposition of "multiculturalism" in educational curricula, and the never-ending crusade against "racism," "sexism," "homophobia," "xenophobia," and "chauvinism." The victory of the globalist agenda would mean in effect the extinction of the United States and its people — not physically, but extinction as a coherent collective identity. That extinction would serve the interests of the globalist elite, for particularist national and cultural institutions restrain the transnational power of the elite and offer impediments to the full scope of its ability to manage the planet. Hence, there is a profound conflict of interest between Americans who want to retain their national identity and those elites, American or not, that seek global unification under their own dominance.

It is likely that this conflict of interest will soon emerge in the United States itself as the principal political and ideological division, replacing or redefining the old division between "right" and "left." Indeed, the conflict is already apparent in the foreign policy of the Bush administration toward emergent nationalisms in Iraq, Yugoslavia, and the Soviet Union. The administration, planning on using existing multinational states as building blocks of the globalist New World Order, is reluctant to recognize the nationalist and ethnic separatist fragmentation of such states. If globalism is to prevail, then its architects cannot allow such centrifugal nationalisms and separatisms to flourish, though even as globalists prophesy the disappearance of nationalism, it explodes under their own noses.

For the most part, the United States has not yet witnessed any such explosion, but sooner or later, as the globalist elites seek to drag the country into conflicts and global commitments, preside over the economic pastoralization of the United States, manage the delegitimization of our own culture and the dispossession of our people, and disregard or diminish our national interests and national sovereignty, a nationalist reaction is almost inevitable and will probably assume populist form when it arrives. The sooner it comes, the better, and if it is to be successful — not merely a militant nostalgia or a hormonal reflex — it will have to define its goals and agendas and the premises on which they are based.

In foreign policy, the idea of putting America first involves a radical dismantling of the Cold War state. It means abrogating most of the mutual defense treaties of the 1950s, withdrawing most of the troops and military bases from Europe and Asia, and terminating almost all foreign aid. It also means that much or most of the national security and foreign policy bureaucracy — in the Pentagon, the State Department, the intelligence community, the U.S. Information Agency, the Agency for International Development, the Peace Corps, etc. — should be abolished or radically reduced in size and functions. Most of these agencies were established for explicitly Cold War purposes, and their continued existence at this point in their present form not only is useless and expensive but also provides a powerful pressure group for continuing globalist adventure and entanglement.

In addition, several conceptual and legal changes are desirable for institutionalizing an America First foreign policy that adequately protects national security and interests in the world but at the same time does not propel us into global management.

(1) Office-holders and candidates for office should be expected to commit themselves to the principle of the national sovereignty and independence of the United States, not only as a legal abstraction but also as a practical guideline for the conduct of foreign and military policy and the approval of treaty commitments. No treaty should be concluded or ratified that compromises or dilutes national sovereignty or requires changes in U.S. law and policy contrary to the Constitution. The Bricker Amendment of the 1950s, which sought to perpetuate these principles in the Constitution itself, should be revived and adopted.

(2) There must be a geopolitical definition of a secure area or perimeter beyond the borders of the United States into which foreign powers would not be allowed to intrude militarily. Pat Buchanan has suggested confining this area to Central America, the Caribbean, and the northern littoral of South America. Not to quibble, but I would expand it to literally hemispheric dimensions, extending from the North Pole to the South and from the Greenwich Meridian to the International Date Line (or geopolitically convenient approximations of these artificial boundaries). Whatever happens within the hemisphere would be deemed relevant to our national security and interests; most of what happens outside it would not be relevant.

(3) The United States should maintain an adequate standing military force to (a) protect its territory and citizens within the hemispheric perimeter and (b) mount rapid and effective punitive and rescue missions outside the perimeter against aggressive powers as needed. The Strategic Defense Initiative

should be implemented, and a standing army and navy should be recruited through universal military training for all able male citizens. The mission of this force should be to fight — not to gain an education, learn a trade, see the world, prove that women are the equals of men, or provide a laboratory for social experiments. Personally, I believe the right to vote should be contingent upon fulfilling the military obligations of the citizen, and this is consistent with the classical republican ideal of a citizens' militia. Foreign aggressors should know that in order to invade the United States, they will have to cut their way through the streets.

(4) There must be a clear recognition of congressional supremacy in foreign affairs, as opposed to the effective executive supremacy that post-Wilsonian liberals and post-Reaganite conservatives have championed. Foreign policy is not different from any other public policy, and there is no reason for the president (i.e., the executive branch bureaucracy) to exercise dictatorial power over it. While the president is the commander-in-chief, negotiates treaties, receives and appoints ambassadors, and is the main consumer of intelligence, every long-term or far-reaching foreign or military commitment must have the support of the American people and the explicit approval of the Congress.

(5) It should be recognized as an explicit principle that no U.S. troops will be committed to combat in the absence of congressional approval and unless military victory is the publicly stated goal. To fight to "contain" an enemy or to fight without using all available resources to assure victory is not acceptable.

(6) Lobbying on behalf of a foreign government or country should be made a federal crime. Foreign governments maintain their own diplomats here to represent their interests, and they don't need Americans to do it for them. Currently, under

the Foreign Agents Registration Act, Americans who represent foreign governments must register with the Justice Department. The registration provision should be repealed, and Americans who prefer the interests of a foreign state to those of their own can either go to the foreign state or go to an American jail.

(7) Perhaps most centrally, the quality of the American population, its education, its economy and technology, and its social disciplines are all, in one sense, "assets" by which the national well-being and security of the country may be measured. They are therefore proper objects of public concern, and while that does not mean that the federal government should manage the population, the economy, education, or social institutions, it does mean that the concept of "America First" implies a nationalist ethic that transcends the preferences and interests of the individual or the interest group and often involves local, state, or federal government action. But the ethic of America First would be a thin one if it were something that only politicians and administrators should respect. It ought to inform the total cultural life of the nation and to be the foundation of our social and cultural identity no less than of our politics and national policies.

Thus, America First trade and immigration policies should recognize that we, as Americans, owe duties to ourselves and our compatriots before we owe anything to other peoples, and restrictions on immigration, free trade, and technology transfer should be debated and framed in terms of our national identity and interests, and not in terms of natural or human rights or the interests of a fictitious "global community." Immigration from countries and cultures that are incompatible with and indigestible to the Euro-American cultural core of the United States should be generally prohibited, current border controls should be rigorously enforced, illegal aliens already here should be rounded up and deported, and employers who hire them should be prosecuted and punished. As for immigrants from less backward countries, we should balance consideration of whatever gains they might bring to our economy with at least equal consideration of their long-term impact on our cultural identity (including our economic and scientific culture). Similar considerations should apply to trade policy; the basic test of free trade or specific restrictions on it should be their consequences for the American national interest, and not whether they promote global economic integration, help less advanced economies, or facilitate individual economic aspirations.

One of the flaws of some of the isolationist and neo-nationalist ideas that have been advanced in the last couple of years is that they recognize no defining principle of American nationality other than the pragmatic and circumstantial ones of economic prosperity and military security. Hence, they are usually unable to define any national interest beyond these goals, and this kind of pragmatic nationalism is unlikely to excite or provide a bond for Americans outside elites professionally interested in economic and military issues. In failing to move beyond pragmatic nationalism, contemporary nationalists neglect the concrete and historical cultural identity of the American nation, express a narrowly defined "national interest" that recognizes only the least common denominator of the national identity, and thereby reflect a similar failing that appeared in the nationalism of Alexander Hamilton.

Hamilton, as his biographer John C. Miller noted, "associated the national government with no great moral issue capable of capturing the popular imagination; he seemed to stand only for 'the natural right of the great fishes to eat up the little ones whenever they can catch them.'" Post-Hamiltonian American nationalism offered no public myth of the nation, and the ultimate price of its failure to do so was the collapse (and subsequent redefinition) of the nation in the Civil War. Only when

Lincoln invested American nationality with a quasi-religious mythology was nationalism politically and popularly successful.

But Lincoln's nationalist myth, drawn from a universalist natural rights egalitarianism, justified national unity only as an instrument of "equality of opportunity" and the acquisitive individualism that follows from it. Lincoln's nationalism soon degenerated into the wolfish egotism of the Gilded Age and the naked imperialism of McKinley and Roosevelt, and ultimately its universalist, egalitarian, and individualist premises contradicted and helped undermine the particularity that a successful nationalism must assert and the subordination of individual ambition that nationalism demands.

If a new nationalism is to flourish and endure, it must do more than offer a merely narrow, pragmatic, and largely economic definition of the national identity and the national interest. It will have to look to the historic norms of the American people and their culture to discover and articulate what America is and what it should be, and it will have to recognize that the American cultural identity involves a good bit more than merely economic growth and individual gratification. If it fails to do so, then the new nationalism will soon become simply one more codeword for the special interests of particular factions and sections, and America will be no more secure, no more prosperous, and no more first than it is today in the custody of its self-serving and self-appointed globalist masters.

[December, 1991]

The Middle-Class Moment

With a whoop and a holler, politicians have suddenly discovered that there's a wild animal called the American middle class prowling around the voting booths, and officeholders are pounding down the stairs to make sure the rough beast does no damage once it gets inside the house. Almost every issue that has emerged in national politics in the last year — term limits and taxes, housing and health care, racial quotas and rascals in government — centers around the cultural identity and material interests of the middle class, and the nation's incumbent oligarchs well understand that all the growling about such matters is rather like the roaring of lions in the jungle night. It's when the roaring stops and the hunt begins that they better start worrying.

The hunt began last fall with the Pyrrhic victory of the oligarchs over David Duke in Louisiana and the announcement soon afterwards of both Mr. Duke and Patrick J. Buchanan of their Middle American-oriented campaigns for President as Republicans. Before that, however, Democrats like Pennsylvania's Harris Wofford and Iowa's Tom Harkin were raising populist banners that the white middle class was likely to find attractive. At the same time, even the oracles of conventional wisdom were beginning to perceive that the middle class was in economic trouble. Columnist George Will, ever a reliable source for what is respectable to think and say, announced his persuasion that middle class economic distress was a significant political force, and *Newsweek* magazine, which is even more conventional if not always as wise as Mr. Will, rehearsed the facts and figures of middle class withering in a cover story the following week. Other journalistic accounts around the same time — in the *Philadelphia Inquirer*, the *New York Times*, and the *Washington Post*, among others — also burrowed into the statistical underbrush to document the same story and sagely pondered its political implications.

The arithmetic of annihilation is by now reasonably familiar. As Mr. Will reported, "The wages of average workers are below 1979 levels, but family incomes have been maintained by wives going to work. In 1960, 30 percent of wives with children under 18 worked. By 1987, 65 percent did. In 1950, the average middle-age middle-class homeowner spent 14 percent of his gross income on mortgage payments. By 1973, that had crept up to 21 percent. In the next 10 years it rocketed to 44 percent. Home ownership rates, which rose for six decades, declined."

The reality of middle class decline is masked by the continuity between the figures for income levels in earlier periods and those for more recent years. The reason for the apparent continuity is that wives are working and thereby bringing in extra income to compensate for what would otherwise be a clear fall in earnings and living standards. The middle class runs faster, expends more energy, to stay in the same place.

Of course, there are the perennial optimists, mostly self-described "conservatives," who make a living out of claiming that the middle class is more prosperous than ever. They like to point to the availability of VCRs, personal computers, and shopping malls to make their case that we've never had it so good. Such cheerleaders seem not to have met Mrs. Margaret Collier of Peoria, Ill., and thousands of wives like her. Mrs. Collier in fact doesn't hold a job, but that's because, as she told the *New York Times*, "It takes me working full-time at home to keep the bills down to the point that we can live on his [Mr.

Collier's] income. I split the wood [for the Franklin stove], plant and work a vegetable garden, can vegetables, buy meat when it is on sale, help my husband fix our cars." Not only does Mrs. Collier not have a personal computer. She seems to live at pretty much the same economic and technological level as an Apache squaw before modern civilization liberated her.

As for home ownership, the Census Bureau reports that today only 9 percent of the nation's renters can afford to buy a home and that 36 percent of actual homeowners would be unable to buy a median-priced home if they had to do so on the market at the time of the survey. To own a home and support a wife who doesn't work are, of course, deeply held aspirations of the American middle class, and the decline of the ability to do so represents a serious economic demotion. It also represents an important social and cultural change. Home ownership — even the abstract and rather fictitious sort of mortgaged ownership to which Americans in recent generations have become habituated — is one of the traditional symbols of the economic and social independence that distinguishes free men from medieval serfs bound to the land or slaves fed from their master's hand. It is difficult to see how the transiency that residential renting involves can be consistent with the kind of rooted commitment to community (or family, for that matter) on which republican government must rely. It is also difficult to understand how family institutions can flourish when wives and mothers must work for a living outside the home. That married women must increasingly do so means fewer children and alternate provisions for existing children — and for preparing meals, shopping, cleaning, etc. Today it means a massive redistribution of social functions and the psychic and moral dislocations that redistribution involves: husbands keeping house, children cooking for themselves, and women escaping the natural bonds of home and husband.

The economic independence of the middle class disappeared long ago, however, when modern corporate and governmental organizations began to swallow the independent businesses and farms that made the bourgeois class of the nineteenth century the core of American society, politics, and culture. At the turn of the century, as historian James Lincoln Collier writes, the middle class constituted "no more than a quarter of the population of the United States," but nevertheless

> it was the dominant section of the social system. It staffed the executive offices of the burgeoning industrial machine, it supplied the majority of office-holders in national, state, and to a lesser extent city governments, it created the art and literature of the time, and perhaps most important, it set the style which those who hoped to rise must follow. In a certain sense this Victorian middle class would — for the moment — decide what America was all about.

The moment did not last long. As Mr. Collier argues, the massive immigration into the United States in the late nineteenth century from Eastern and Southern Europe introduced alien subcultural fragments into a largely Anglo-Saxon culture, and the immigrants "were bringing to the United States an array of habits, attitudes, and folkways that conflicted, at times dramatically, with the prevailing American patterns of thought and behavior. They were, in sum, resolutely anti-Victorian in almost every respect. They did not believe in discipline, punctuality, sobriety — the order and decency of the Victorian ethic," which was also a middle class ethic, and as new immigrants rose socially and economically, especially through the mass entertainment industry they helped create, they displaced the Victorian ethic with their own anti-bourgeois patterns of living.

The "Victorian ethic" was itself a code well-adapted to an entrepreneurial society of independent, self-governing bourgeois, but it was a code that could not serve the mass organizations of corporation and state, union and political party, that were displacing the compact, autonomous, and decentralized institutions of the old republic. Absorbed within these organizations as workers, consumers, and largely passive audiences and voters, the American middle class ceased to be either independent or dominant, and it increasingly took on the characteristics of a proletariat, despite the affluence that it retained.

Middle class affluence was itself preserved by the engines of managerial capitalism in close alliance with the administrative state, and if the middle class fought the wars and paid the taxes for the emerging leviathan, it also received no small share of the material benefits in the form of farm subsidies, small business loans, education through the G.I. Bill, housing policy, and union legislation. Having gained material security through its dependence on the managerial system, however, the middle class ceased to be both independent as well as the dominant and defining core of American society, and the bourgeois ethic of the nineteenth century slowly began to wither. By the 1950s, television's situation comedies and the dreadful instructional films that warned teenagers of the perils of drugs, sex, drinking, rock and roll, and reckless driving recorded the lame efforts of a deracinated and dislocated middle class desperately trying to transmit its codes to to its progeny and pathetically proving that it had not the slightest idea of how to do so.

Yet today even the moment of material security that the middle class enjoyed has proved fleeting, and what is occurring in the economy now is the final stage of proletarianization and dispossession before the middle class disappears forever as a distinct stratum of society. Fragments of the bourgeois ethic survive and provide a makeshift ideological framework for the middle class revolt now bubbling in the suburbs and housing developments, but what feeds the revolt is not so much any fierce attachment to the Victorian ethic or the old republic it served as a demand for the kind of material security the post-bourgeois middle class once enjoyed.

What the leaders of the revolt must do is understand and make clear to their potential following that that kind of security cannot be restored unless those who demand it have gained sufficient political and cultural power to become again the defining core of the whole society and to identify the national interest with their own social interests and identity. But such political and cultural power can be gained only if the post-bourgeois middle class is able and willing to form a distinct social and political identity separate from the old bourgeois middle class and in opposition to the incumbent elites in the state, economy, and culture. Today the middle class has too many competitors in the underclass and its elite allies for the material benefits of the mega-state to expect to retain the benefits it once enjoyed without a struggle for power. Moreover, the current elites not only don't care about the economic security of the American middle class (or of America); they welcome its decline and destruction. The *New York Times*, in its account of the plight of the Peoria middle class, quotes Chairman Donald V. Fites of Caterpillar, Inc., the industrial mainstay of Peoria, that "There is a narrowing of the gap between the average American's income and that of the Mexicans. As a human being, I think what is going on is positive. I don't think it is realistic for 250 million Americans to control so much of the world's G.N.P." With leaders like Mr. Fites, the average American would be better off swimming the Rio Grande and seeking welfare in Matamoros. Only if the post-bourgeois stratum aspires to displace the incumbent elite, dismantle its apparatus of power, and itself constitute a new elite and re-constitute American society can it expect to restore its own security, preserve itself from destruction, and extend its present moment in the political sun into an enduring epoch of civilization.

[March, 1992]

The Jungle of Empire

One of the redeeming features of imperialism is that it makes for great adventure stories. The works of H. Rider Haggard and Rudyard Kipling and the literature of the American West from James Fenimore Cooper to Louis L'Amour would not have been possible without the empires and imperial problems that provide the setting for their tales. The reason for the relationship ought to be fairly obvious.

Empires offer all the standard fare of blood, guts, intrigue, romance, and action: villains plotting to overthrow civilization, heroes striving to protect it; crumbling cultures and uncharted jungles that house mystery, danger, and immense rewards for those bold enough to seize them. Empires may make deserts and call them peace, but at least they also offer a lot of entertainment that sometimes lasts longer than the civilization that imagines it is perpetuating itself through territorial expansion.

Today we still have empires, or at least one, but the literature it spawns makes the penny dreadfuls and potboilers of the Victorian era seem like the stuff of Homer and Virgil. I can think of no great adventure tale to emerge from the consolidation of what may turn out to be the largest transnational apparatus of power yet to appear in history, and the cosmopolites of the American megapower will have to make do with Stephen King and Tom Clancy. The best spy novels produced by the Cold War, such as those of John LeCarre, so far from celebrating empire, in fact are somber introspections on what power demands of human beings and what it takes from them.

It is precisely because contemporary globalism is so uninspiring and because its power is not acquired through the combined exertions of muscle, bone, and brain that it produces few compelling tales of what it cost to create. Indeed, the costs of modern imperialism, like the bonds that hold it together, remain invisible. Unlike the regimes constructed by the British, the Romans, or the Macedonians, the one that flutters about the world today was not built on force and human risk but on an entirely different kind of power.

Machiavelli distinguished between two kinds of rulers. There are those who, imitating lions, base their power on force, and those, imitating foxes, who base it on cunning. Ideally, in so far as Machiavelli permitted himself ideals, a ruler ought to combine the two traits, but he recognized that human psychology being what it is, few potentates were capable of doing so for very long. Several centuries after Machiavelli, another Italian, Vilfredo Pareto, revived his distinction and elaborated it into an entire psychology of power.

Pareto discussed two classes of what he called "residues," his term for basic instinctual drives that underlie human behavior. "Class I," as he called one group of residues, consists of "the instinct for combinations," and those in whom it is strong tend to be innovative and manipulative, or, in a word, cunning. They tend to respond to problems by "combining" different elements — ideas, people, institutions, resources — to produce new instruments that resolve the problem.

Residues of "Class II" or the "instinct for the persistence of aggregates," on the other hand, yield behavior that is socially conservative. Those in whom they are powerful dislike and avoid change — their ideas and behavioral habits are "aggregates" that tend to "persist" — and they typically respond to problems by appeals to group solidarity. Hence, family, race,

class, nation, community, religious sect, and other group identities are important bonds for those in whom Class II residues
are strong. They tend to avoid innovation and manipulation
and, like lions, to rely on force to deal with problems.

In some societies, Pareto argued, Class I residues (or the
people in whom they are dominant) rise to the top, while in
others, Class II types emerge. Whichever type emerges, it
forms an elite and seeks to perpetuate its power and construct a
society that reflects and supports its mentality and habits. Pareto
believed that ancient Athens in its so-called "Golden Age" of
empire and cultural brilliance was a rather good example of a
Class I manipulative regime, in which commercial classes, political demagoguery, and intellectual and artistic expression were
prevalent, while Sparta in the same period was a classic case of
a Class II or "leonine" elite: unimaginative, strongly attached
to traditional identities, and relying on force. His typology
corresponds more or less to what Aristotle said of the two societies, and the Greek philosopher argued that the weakness of
Sparta was that it recognized only "one kind of goodness,"
namely skill in war.

To Pareto, a lion was not necessarily better or worse than
a fox, and like Machiavelli (or Aristotle), he believed that a
human being or a ruler or a society in which one kind of resi-
due was predominant to the exclusion of the other was particularly weak. Since each type tends to respond to problems and
challenges only by means of the behavior, attitudes, and ideas
that its dominant instinct recognizes, it is unable to deal with
crises on which such responses don't work.

Hence, a society or a regime in which foxes are predominant will be unable to prosecute wars effectively or respond to
challenges from enemies that rely on force. Similarly, a society or a regime in which lions are the dominant class will tend
to stagnate and to meet every challenge with force, sometimes

brutally. Sooner or later, the habitual responses of each type fail to work. Sooner or later, each type runs into problems that its characteristic style of behavior and thought can't solve, and it is overwhelmed. The result is the fall of one elite and the rise of another, leading Pareto to comment in a famous phrase that "history is a graveyard of aristocracies" or elites.

Pareto did not know or talk much about the United States in the nineteenth century, but if he had, he might have enjoyed himself. There he would have seen a protracted social conflict between two kinds of societies — one, based in the American South and later in the West, that was strongly attached to such social groupings as community, region, family, race, and nation, and the other, based in the Northeast, that was innovative, more loosely attached to elemental social bonds and identities, and resembled in some ways the Athens of the Golden Age. The conflict between the two was resolved in the American Civil War, when the Northeastern foxes destroyed the Southern lions, though they did so not so much through their skill in war as through their successful and often brilliant manipulation of their economic and technological resources.

Having suppressed the challenge from the lions, however, the foxes of the Northeast proceeded to mold American society into a form more suitable to their continued power. Commercial, industrial, and technological skills became a main avenue to wealth and political power. Demagoguery, the manipulation of the population through patronage and the techniques of mass democracy, became a standard feature of American politics. Culturally, the ideologies of the era centered around the favorite themes of foxes: progress, individualism, innovation, opportunity, acquisition of wealth.

Eventually, the dominant groups in the new nation were destroyed by their own success. Having built up large organizations that relied on the manipulative skills of managers, not even the victors in the social and political revolution of the Civil War could hold on to the reins of power when corporations, mass political parties, unions, governmental bureaucracies, and mass universities and foundations replaced the smaller-scale institutions of bourgeois America. Lacking the instinctual group bonds and loyalties that characterize lions, the bourgeois foxes never knew what hit them, and to this day most of them still don't.

What has emerged in the twentieth century is no less an imperial regime than those run by the Romans or the British, but unlike those empires, the managerial hegemony today is founded on the manipulative proclivities and skills of foxes. Hence, the elite of the imperial system thinks of social problems and challenges only in terms of manipulation. Instead of punishment for criminals, they respond with rehabilitation and therapy. Instead of war with foreign enemies, they try negotiations, foreign aid, exporting democracy, and applied social engineering. Instead of bluntly repressing domestic rivals and rebels, they meet them with discussion and social reconstruction to remove the "root causes" of discontent.

For all the murky conspiracy theories concocted by the left about the "power elite" that supposedly plotted the murder of John F. Kennedy, clobbered the New Left, and leapt into the Vietnam war in a fit of nineteenth century imperialism, the left has succeeded in grandly missing the point of the very regime it purports to oppose. The managerial regime doesn't assassinate much of anybody, and when it tries, as it did in the early 1960s, its efforts look like something out of "Get Smart." Exploding cigars and poisoned wetsuits were the weapons the CIA presented as the devices for the assassination of Fidel Castro, and with enemies like the pot-bellied spooks of Langley, the caudillo of Havana could expect to live to a ripe old age. The Black Panthers and the Weathermen of the '60's ran into trouble only when they encountered local and state police less attuned to the devices of the Higher Repression designed by the marshals of the managerial state, which simply rounded up the rebels, listened to their whines and bitches, and then sent them home to become TV celebrities and real estate tycoons. Having locked the malcontents into the pleasures of a managerial system that manipulates and dominates even as it rewards and entertains, the elite had nothing more to fear from the left, new or old.

As for war, foxes don't much care for it, though when they engage in it, as Pareto noted, "the sword is rattled only before the weak." The managerial regime has so far rattled its sword and thumped its chest in Vietnam, Grenada, Libya, Panama, and Iraq, while stronger powers such as the late and unlamented Soviet Union that conquer whole continents and massacre entire plane loads of civilians are too tightly locked into the global system of management to be the target of serious military force. What is striking about the way in which the managerial system "fought" the Cold War is not that the threat was contrived or invented but that, despite the reality of Soviet aggression and subversion, the Western managerial states did so little to confront and resolve the threat. It was never war but merely preparation for war that the system and its managers cared for, and the real purpose of all the vast apparatus of armies, navies, planes, bombs, and missiles was not to defend the West in war with communism but to enhance the domestic power of those who designed, bought, built, and managed them and the bureaucracies that produced them.

Instead of war and repression through force, the managerial system relies on the manipulative arts of modern communications, public administration, advertising, propaganda, and mass entertainment. In order to extend its reach to the fullest, it has to break down the institutional bonds and beliefs that resist such manipulation, and hence it undermines family, class, property, community, religious sects, and racial and ethnic identities.

Having perfected the manipulative arts to global scale, it is now in the process of extending its dominion to the entire world, actually disengaging from its territorial base in the nation-state and constructing a transnational apparatus of power by which nations and their populations, resources, and cultures can be managed. There is a good deal of talk about how computers and other post-industrial technologies will lead to a radical decentralization of organizations. Don't bet on it. The technology works both ways. It can be used to promote decentralization, but it also lends itself to tighter control from the center. Human nature seems to prefer more power and less responsibility, and my own bet is that post-industrial technologies will accommodate that preference.

The question, of course, is: Will it last? Will human nature prove to be so easily manipulable that elites dedicated to infinite and eternal manipulation endure? If Pareto's analysis of the psychological anatomy of the regime of foxes is useful in understanding how and why it operates the way it does, his view of how it crumbles is also suggestive. The process of decline is almost Hegelian in its dialectic. Sooner or later, a regime based on the application of force and appeal to collective solidarity withers in the face of challenges to which its elite is unable to respond, given its own psychological and behavioral tendencies. Last year this is exactly what happened to the Soviet Union, when its elite, utterly clueless as to the nature of the crises its regime was encountering and utterly unable to manipulate its way out of these crises, collapsed rather like the wonderful one hoss shay.

By the same argument, sooner or later a regime based almost purely on manipulation and its arts will encounter challenges that just can't be manipulated. Last year also, the American managerial system ran into exactly that sort of problem in Saddam Hussein, who simply ignored all the negotiations, threats, and peace marches mounted by his adversaries and who even succeeded in ignoring his adversaries' devastating military victory. But sooner or later also, a manipulative regime will even run into a challenge that it not only can't manipulate but also can't devastate, and when that happens, the manipulative regime crumbles no less quickly than its counterpart based on force. This is not a happy situation, but, if Pareto is right, it seems to be a law of history. At least it makes for exciting adventure stories.

[April, 1992]

New World Baseball

For all of the subtle grace that distinguishes Japanese civilization, the esoteric gabble of Western diplomacy seems to elude its leaders. Every few months, some titan of Tokyo pronounces his low opinion of America and Americans, unveiling his view that our schools are dreadful, our racial minorities backward, our politicians crooks, or our workers lazy.

Where they get such ideas I can't imagine, but unlike Americans themselves, the Japanese appear to be incapable of being trained to shut up about them. Yankees have long since learned that to utter such insights is to commit political and professional suicide. No small amount of the resentment Americans express at such attitudes may arise from their realization that our society is by no means as "open" as its high priests like to boast. Only madmen and barbarians may speak the truth and get out alive.

Last winter Japanese Prime Minister Kiichi Miyazawa, who entered office professing his admiration for the United States, loosed his lips on the floor of the Japanese Diet to the effect that he suspected that Americans "may lack a work ethic," and from the wrath his remarks inspired, you would have thought he had ordained a second attack on Pearl Harbor. President Bush had some sharp rejoinders to the crack in his State of the Union address, and in Detroit the United Auto Workers responded by setting up a Japanese car in their offices and encouraging visitors to pulverize it with sledgehammers.

But not all Americans were displeased with the Japanese. A few days after Mr. Miyazawa's musings, the city of Seattle revealed that its leaders were promoting an agreement with the Japanese chairman of Nintendo to buy the local baseball team. Seattle's mayor, the governor of Washington, and Sen. Slade Gorton all joined to induce the baseball commissioner to let the deal go down.

The people of Seattle themselves seemed to be enchanted with the idea and openly resentful of the attempt by the rest of America to think harshly of our friends across the sea. The *New York Times* quoted Seattle longshoreman Ron Thornberry that "I'm personally not that happy with what they've been saying about our workers in Japan, but I do know that if America were to have some sort of protectionism against them, it would kill us."

Mr. Thornberry's sentiments make sense from the point of view of his own and his region's economic interests. The area around Seattle is heavily dependent on trade with Asia. Asians are the fastest growing minority in the state, and for the last decade state officials have eagerly courted Japanese investment. Nevertheless, the longshoreman's response illustrates what is wrong with free trade and, with all due respect to our self-appointed social critics in Tokyo, with Americans who become addicted to it.

Free trade is not so much an economic policy as it is a political ideology. As economist William Hawkins has argued in a number of articles over the last decade, the free trade ideology was an integral part of 19th century liberalism and its explicit rejection of the idea of the nation, the state, society, and the group. In the happy world of classical liberal ideology, writes Mr. Hawkins,

> Economics was to be separated from politics, wealth from power. Liberals viewed people as equal individuals, not as members of particular national states. Civil society's only valid activity was the protection of individual rights; the nation-state had no independent status or mystical nature

to which individuals owed any allegiance or duty that entailed any sacrifice of narrow self interest. There would be no national interests, indeed no international relations — only "citizens of the world" going about their private affairs.

It follows from the ideology of free trade that there is no "national interest" in economics; there are only the interests of individuals. Hence, there is no way for the government to identify an economic policy that will reflect its national interests and no reason why it should do so, and when, in the give and take of commerce, another nation begins to devour parts of your own country to the point that the residents of those parts come to prefer the other country, there is nothing anyone can or should do about it. The logical — and today, the actual — result of free trade carried out as an ideology is the economic and eventually the political dismemberment of the nation that practices it.

Proponents of unlimited free trade with Japan try to counter this argument by claiming that Japanese investment in the United States is really much lower than what its opponents claim. They point out that Great Britain is the single largest foreign owner of American assets ($98.9 billion as opposed to Japan's $84.8 billion) and that the total domestic net worth of foreign ownership in this country is merely 5 percent of Gross Domestic Product.

Unhappily, they miss the point, which is that European states are not aggressively pursuing the acquisition of assets in the United States. Japan is. As economist Douglas P. Woodward writes, "Japanese companies have advanced more rapidly than any other source, with an annual growth rate (42 percent) far exceeding all major investor nations during the 1980s. In 1980, Japan held the seventh largest position. By the decade's close it had vaulted to second place, with $69.7 billion of U.S. holdings — 17 percent of the total. The gross product of Japanese-affiliated companies in the United States also grew faster than any other nation from 1977-1987, but remained below the

United Kingdom and Canada."

The state of Washington is one part of the United States where the Japanese seem to have made real progress, and the dialectic of free trade swings low over the whole Northwest. As the *New York Times* reported, "Increasingly, the American Northwest, along with British Columbia and Alberta in Canada, is trying to market itself to the world economy as a single economic unit, calling itself Cascadia." The region includes Alaska, Washington, Oregon, Montana, Idaho, and the two Canadian provinces, and it "'stands at the very geographical center of the new economic order', said Paul Schell, a Seattle port commissioner. International boundaries, he said, mean very little."

Just so. While Americans bemuse themselves that they have no collective economic interest, Japan has long since liberated itself from such 19th century superstition and is aggressively pursuing policies intended to enhance not only its own wealth but also its power. It may not actually plan to dismember the United States and Canada, but the long-term effect of its policies is to promote just that. As the fortunes of "Cascadians" fall hostage to the well-being of Japan and other Asian nations, so will their affections and their loyalties, and eventually political identity will go with them. Of course, there's no reason to think that the artificial "unit" of Cascadia will endure, any more than any other political unit founded merely on economic self-interest will last. As soon as patterns of trade, technology, and ownership change, Cascadia itself can be expected to disappear through the fiber optic tubes of the New World economy.

It is entirely appropriate that ownership of the local baseball team should be the immediate reason for Seattle's love affair with Tokyo. The chairman of Nintendo no doubt understands that what a lot of Americans in the New World economic order really want is not national sovereignty or the protection of their national economic interests and identity but fun.

Unwilling or unable to support their own baseball team, the good human resources of Seattle are perfectly happy to let the Japanese provide it for them, and anybody who challenges the offer is simply not a fun-loving American, let alone a productive resource.

If the ideology of free trade recognizes only individuals and their interests, it also implies that the only interests that matter even for individuals are those connected to consumption, and consumption in the post-industrial economic culture means fun. As long as Americans can cough up credit cards, live from paycheck to paycheck, survive on junk food, and stack their attics with every video game, electronic toy, and New Age gadget the wizards of Nintendo can weld together, what difference does it make how they earn a living? The slogan — perhaps the epitaph — of free trade logic is the *bon mot* reportedly uttered by one of its major champions in the Bush administration, Council of Economic Advisers Chairman Michael Boskin. Informed by critics of free trade that the Japanese were systematically taking over the U.S. microchip industry, Mr. Boskin replied, "Potato chips, computer chips, what's the difference? They're all chips. A hundred dollars worth of one or a hundred dollars worth of the other is still a hundred dollars."

Mr. Boskin is correct that a worker who makes a hundred dollars producing potato chips is earning the same as one who earns a hundred dollars making computer chips, and each worker can use his earnings to buy whatever gadgets he wants (except American computer chips). From the point of view of the individual as consumer, there is no difference. But from the point of view of the society or the nation, there is, the most obvious being that Patriot missiles and the other high-tech toys of modern war don't run on potato chips.

National security alone thus refutes free trade ideology simply because the ability to muster the technical power necessary to protect national security contains and always will contain an economic component, and limitations on trade on the basis of defense considerations have been recognized as legitimate even by the architects of free trade since the days of Adam Smith.

But national security is not the only constraint on foreign trade and investment. There is also the matter of what we want to be and can be as a nation. After all, Haiti can produce potato chips, but it will be a long time before its population is able to turn out a computer chip, let alone design a better one. Free trade ideologues like Mr. Boskin believe Americans ought to be contented cattle happily punching buttons on the assembly lines in an economy based on fun and immediate gratification, but my bet is that he'd rather his own kids learned more about making chips for computers than slicing potatoes. At this historical moment, the design and production of computers happens to be the culminating pinnacle of Western and American science and engineering, and to claim that it makes no difference if we lose our ability to continue it is as much a renunciation of our identity and our heritage as teaching our children that Cleopatra was black.

Free trade doctrinaires, of course, care nothing for that identity and heritage if they can't think of a way to sell it, eat it, or copulate with it. In their economic vision, not only all human beings but all economic interests are equal, and none is entitled to special protection any more than any other. But as with egalitarian ideology applied to men and women, so with the same superstition applied to economic products. In the real world, some men and women are better than others and more deserving of protection, and some economic products, skills, and ideas are worth more than others. Contrary to Jeremy Bentham, a father of free trade ideology, there is a difference between pushpin and poetry, and there is also a difference between computer chips and potato chips.

Classical liberal economics certainly has its merits, but it and its parent political ideology have long since been discarded in almost every aspect of economic policy except trade. It just so happens that it is the free trade part of classical liberalism that comports well with the interests of emerging transnational elites. Bureaucrats at the United Nations and the other transnational institutions that speckle the horizon, the managers and investors of multinational corporations that depend on trade with foreign nations and have ceased to be American in any sense other than their post office boxes, and the tribe of lobbyists that haunts the District of Columbia (and the campaigns of almost all this year's presidential candidates) all stand to make more money and gain more power through policies that promote the dismemberment of the United States through free trade (and through massive immigration and political denationalization) than by strong affirmations of national interests and identity. Through their combined economic and political interests, they have begun to disengage from the underlying soil of their nations and cultures and to form a new block of interests that transcends national boundaries. To them, as Mr. Schell avers, international boundaries "mean very little."

What global free trade and the other instruments of denationalization promise, therefore, is not the "end of history" or the triumph of democratic capitalism forever and ever or a "neutral" or "minimal" state umpiring a "level playing field." What marches in their train is the emergence of a new world power bloc separated from and in contradiction to the power, interests, and civilization of particular nation states and the prospect that the new transnational power will eventually preside over the decomposition of nations. How long the new elite will let us play baseball in its new regime is a question most Americans have not yet begun to ask.

[May, 1992]

The Buchanan Revolution — Part I

Nothing churns the entrails of the professional democracy priesthood more than the rancid taste of a little real democracy. Since one of the main dishes on the 1992 political menu has been a generous serving of authentic popular rebellion, the sages have spent a good part of the last year lurching for their lavatories. The very same brahmins who demand democracy in all its terrors in Peru and South Africa turned green at the prospect of Americans actually beginning to think about and support candidates, parties, and ideas all by themselves, and the self-appointed caste that tries to make sure nobody gets to see the wizards who run the country in the Emerald Cities of Washington and New York put their noggins together to keep the masses at bay.

Having worked themselves into a lather over David Duke all fall, the brahmins were disappointed that the former Klansman did not provide more sport once the campaign actually began, but the venom they had stored in their fangs for Mr. Duke they spent instead on what they took to be a reasonable facsimile in the person of Patrick J. Buchanan. Perennial Men of the People such as Jerry Brown and Tom Harkin inspired only amusement, but Mr. Buchanan's candidacy unleashed a flood of poison that rose higher every time he kissed another baby.

Nevertheless, though Mr. Buchanan never won a primary, he was the undoubted star of the presidential campaign, and what he did accomplish is something that few if any professional politicians have achieved since World War II. It is rare that any candidate challenging an incumbent president gains more than 10 to 12 percent of the popular vote in his own party's primaries, but there are some precedents for it. What is unheard of is for a challenger who is not a professional politician to win that many votes and indeed to take no less than a third of his party's supporters against a sitting chief executive. Mr. Buchanan has never held public office and has never before run for election for anything, yet in the primaries through Super-Tuesday, he consistently won more than 30 percent of the vote against a man who has spent his entire life flapping from one public nest to another and who a year before had enjoyed such high levels of popular favor that those Americans who didn't support him probably didn't know who the president was.

The conventional brahminical interpretation of the Buchanan following is that it was a "protest vote," a phrase that explains little and raises several more questions than it answers. "Protest" against what exactly, and why should any large number of voters be disposed to protest? To be sure, there are perpetual malcontents in every party who are ever disposed to vote against whoever holds office, but no serious political observer believes that they compose anything like a third of a major party that has held the White House for 12 years.

The reason for Mr. Buchanan's strong showing in the primaries is closely related to the reasons for the extraordinarily poisonous verbiage directed at him from the day he announced his candidacy. Indeed, the one is a kind of mirror image of the other, for it was exactly what attracted the rank-and-file voters to him that repelled the brahmins and their entourage. Of course, there were several different specific elements that fed the smear campaign against him. Zionists and many American Jews appeared to be obsessed by the delusion that Mr. Buchanan was

an anti-Semite, had denied that the slaughter of Jews by the
Nazis had occurred, and had expressed admiration for Adolf
Hitler. For obvious political reasons, the Bush administration,
usually on the sly, seized every opportunity to encourage such
lies, even as Mr. Bush and Secretary of State James Baker
were raked by similar accusations because of their opposition
to Israeli housing policy in the West Bank.

In addition to the prepossessions of some Jewish obsessives
such as Abe Rosenthal, Norman Podhoretz, and Charles
Krauthammer (but by no means all or even the general run of
Jews, since some of Mr. Buchanan's most outspoken defenders
against these lies were themselves Jewish, such as *Human
Events'* Allan Ryskind, Murray Rothbard, Paul Gottfried, Robert
Novak, and Michael Kinsley), there was the general fury directed by the left against any serious conservative or anti-liberal. In this respect, the vilification crusade against Mr. Buchanan was not qualitatively different from those of the past directed against Joe McCarthy, Richard Nixon, Barry Goldwater,
Ronald Reagan, and Jesse Helms.

But the canards cast at Buchanan reached a pitch that earlier ones tossed at prominent conservatives had never attained,
and when supposed conservative leaders such as William Bennett
and Newt Gingrich joined in the baying of the pack, it was
clear that something different was going on and that the authors
of these mendacities had perceived some quality in the Buchanan movement that disturbed them more than usual.

What they perceived was in fact the emergence of a new
identity in American politics, one that the high science of managed and manipulated democracy is not yet quite prepared to
handle and which is therefore more of a threat to the established powers than almost any previous challenge from the right
or left. Despite his background as the nation's most prominent
conservative commentator, Mr. Buchanan presented himself as

a bit more than a conventional conservative candidate, and the really significant aspects of his campaign were precisely those that departed from the mainstream of what has declaimed itself as conservatism in recent years. The themes of "America First" and the "Middle American Revolution" that Mr. Buchanan articulated appealed to a particular identity, embodied in the concepts of America as a nation with discrete national political and economic interests and of the Middle American stratum as the political, economic, and cultural core of the nation. In adopting such themes, Mr. Buchanan decisively broke with the universalist and cosmopolitan ideology that has been masquerading as conservatism and which has marched up and down the land armed with a variety of universalist slogans and standards: natural rights; equality as a conservative principle; the export of global democracy as the primary goal of American foreign policy; unqualified support for much of the civil rights agenda, unlimited immigration, and free trade; the defense of one version or another of "one-worldism"; enthusiastic worship of an abstract "opportunity" and unrestricted economic growth through acquisitive individualism; and the adulation of the purported patron saints of all these causes in the persons of Abraham Lincoln and Martin Luther King, Jr.

None of these idols has much to do with the central task of an authentic conservatism, which is the survival and enhancement of a particular people and its institutionalized cultural expressions. All of them are instead universalist banners that can be fluttered by Pakistanis and Patagonians as easily as by Americans, and whatever their merits (which are very few) there is nothing in them that distinguishes us as a particular people, a particular nation, or a particular culture. Collectively they constitute what Professor Claes Ryn of Catholic University has recently called the "New Jacobinism," and it is hardly accidental that their more literate exponents (such as Allan Bloom) explicitly and properly root their creed in the Enlightenment of the eighteenth century, an era that historically has been repugnant to traditional conservatism but is intimately embraced by the universalist cosmo-conservatives.

Nor is it surprising that the political left is enchanted by this redefinition of the right in universalist terms, since the redefinition promises a right that is philosophically indistinguishable from the left itself, a right that can sooner or later (probably sooner) be pushed to the same practical political conclusions that the left has reached from the same premises, at which point there will be no serious ideological opposition to the left and its dominance at all.

Hence, both the left and the cosmo-conservatives were eager to join forces in trying to muzzle Mr. Buchanan's "New Nationalism" as soon as it began to bark, for they correctly saw it as a threat to the cultural uniformity and hegemony that the left and the universalist right demand for themselves, and it was the anti-universalist aspects of Mr. Buchanan's message that informed the most notorious denunciation of him by Mr. Bennett last winter. Mr. Bennett's accusation, in response to a question from George Will, was provoked by a column by Mr. Krauthammer attacking Mr. Buchanan, and the whole trio of cosmo-conservatives denounced Mr. Buchanan's "flirting with fascism" — that is, his assertions of economic nationalism, his criticisms of unrestricted immigration, and his supposed "racism" in criticizing Israel and defending a foreign policy centered on American national interests. To cosmo-conservatism, this is precisely what fascism is, the invocation of the claims of the particular over those of the universal.

In an earlier column, Mr. Will had criticized Mr. Buchanan for failing to "understand what distinguishes American nationality." "Ours," Mr. Will intoned, "is, as the first Republican president said, a nation dedicated to a proposition."

It is the characteristic proposition of political universalism that
the heritage and meaning of historically distinct nations, cultures, and peoples can be captured in and by propositions that
are universal in their application, and the rejection of such propositions is to the universalist mind at best tribalism and at worst
the bricks of which gas chambers are built. The inconvenient
historical truth is that genocide and modern ideological tyranny
have far more often been the product of universalism itself,
especially its egalitarian incarnations, than any assertion of particularist loyalties and identity.

But the main threat presented by Mr. Buchanan and his
own tribe was not merely their expression of an anti-universalist doctrine and agenda but the wide appeal these expressions
enjoyed. The irony of the New Nationalism is that its explicit
particularist and nationalist appeal to distinctively Middle American values and interests lifts it out of the ghettoes and cloisters
that have been the natural habitat of the American right since
World War II. Mr. Buchanan suddenly found himself speaking to sympathetic audiences of factory workers, students, and
middle-income voters whose interest in and comprehension of
the esoterica of conservative metaphysics has always been as
minimal as their commitment to the sonorities of the left. For
the first time since the Depression perhaps, there loomed the
prospect of a unified people transcending the artificial and obsolete framework of right and left and militantly intent on dis-
lodging the reigning elites to take power back to their own
bosoms for their own purposes. Today this is known as "fascism"; it used to be called "democracy," which is the real reason the left-right establishment is so frightened by it.

Yet in the end, for all their lies, there is not a great deal the
incumbent elites can do about Buchananism, and they must be
experiencing much the same exhilarating emotions that French
and Russian aristocrats enjoyed when they listened to the som-

ber sounds of tumbrels in the streets of Paris and St. Petersburg. No one imagined that their campaign of vilification had much political consequence, and it was mainly through reliance on the natural advantages of presidential incumbency that the Buchanan revolution was momentarily frustrated. But no one should imagine either that the revolution is over. Indeed, Mr. Buchanan's presidential campaign was only the opening shot, and whether he runs again or does or does not eventually win the White House, he has unleashed a force in American politics that cannot be bridled. Its main mission now is to embark on a long march that will popularize and legitimize its claims to be the vehicle of a reborn national consciousness, and that mission is only in part political in the narrow sense. As a great global democrat once said, a house divided against itself cannot stand, and the main message of the Middle American Revolution is that the real masters of the house are ready to repossess it and drive out the usurpers.

[July, 1992]

The Buchanan Revolution — Part II

Perhaps the greatest irony of the periodic political revolutions that occur in American democracy is that most of the voters who make them possible have not the foggiest notion of what they are doing. In 1932, Franklin Roosevelt won the White House by running on a platform that promised to balance the budget and reduce the scale and power of the federal government, and there is no doubt that most of the Americans who sent him to Washington supported him simply because of the desperate economic straits in which they found themselves and their country, not because of any passion they shared with him for the socialist and internationalist experiments that he and his brood immediately imposed. The same could probably be said for almost all the major presidential elections in our history. The truth is that the concepts of the "people's will" and the "mandate" are largely political fictions that serve to mask the ambitions and intrigues of the small cadres who really run governments at all times, regardless of the forms and rhetorical dressing these elites assume.

The same is true of the Buchanan revolution of the 1990s, and the claim by its opponents that most of the voters who supported Mr. Buchanan in the Republican primaries did so as a "protest vote" and not because of any serious endorsement of the candidate's ideas is thus largely irrelevant, even if true. Let us say that only some 10 percent of the average 30 percent vote Mr. Buchanan received before Super Tuesday this year

actually agreed with his ideas, while the others who voted for
him were merely protesting the state of the economy and the
lackluster leadership of the incumbent or simply pulled the wrong
lever or got Pat Buchanan mixed up with the predecessor of
Abraham Lincoln. That means that Mr. Buchanan's meaningful support was still comparable to the total vote received by
one of his principal ideological rivals, Jack Kemp, whose average take of the Republican primary vote in 1988 was less than 5
percent. Nevertheless, the fans of Mr. Kemp to this day actually believe that his eagerness to redefine conservatism so as to
win the plaudits of the left and the urban underclass is just the
ticket for the political future, both within the Republican Party
as well as in the country at large. You may not have to fool all
the people all the time in order to make a political revolution,
but you do have to befuddle more than one out of twenty. So
far only Mr. Buchanan has been able to come close to building
a new national political coalition that not only offers an alternative to President Bush's centrist establishmentarianism but also
seeks to articulate a political myth that can bridge or transcend
the obsolete categories of right and left entirely.

What has happened in the Buchanan revolution, as I argued in this space last month, is the emergence of a new political identity that focuses on the concrete and particular interests
and beliefs of the nation and of a particular social, cultural, and
political force — Middle America — as the defining core of the
nation. Mr. Buchanan was by no means the first to give political expression to this force, and he may not be the one who
carries it to a successful revolutionary fulfillment. Perhaps it
was David Duke who actually initiated it in recent times, and
perhaps it will be H. Ross Perot who brings it to fruition. But
Mr. Duke, for obvious reasons, was not an acceptable spokesman, and Mr. Perot, for all the charm of his accent, will probably be unable to accomplish its agenda. The Texas billionaire

has all the political sophistication of a man who watches the *Today* show at least three times a week and believes everything he hears on it, and his unwillingness or inability to tell anyone what he would actually do about the various crises he has cribbed from television and weekly news magazines suggests that he would be quickly devoured by existing political elites if he really arrived in Washington. Mr. Perot displays the typical naivete of businessmen, who always suffer under the delusion that government operates just like the enterprises they and their golfing partners command. He may succeed in winning the Buchanan vote, and he may win the White House, but if he does, he will discover that giving orders to Congress, federal officials, lobbies, interest groups, and foreign powers is not the same as peddling computers and telling his secretaries to retype his letters.

Yet regardless of who began it and who will finish it, the Middle American Revolution is not going to go away. None of its political leaders created the social movement on which it rests, and it will survive their own personalities and campaigns. Indeed, it was predictable as long ago as the early Reagan administration that something like the movement would emerge sooner or later and that it would displace "conservatism," if not also "liberalism."

The Reagan movement also was to a large extent a political expression of the economic and cultural frustrations of Middle Americans, but no sooner had Mr. Reagan settled himself in the White House than his administration was invaded and largely captured by what may generally be called the "Soft Right" — not only neo-conservatives but also the Republican Establishment and the whole swarm of Court Conservatives who merely sought employment of their otherwise unemployable talents in the vast public relief system known as the federal government. The Court Conservatives included almost all of the policy eggheads, direct mail tycoons, 50-year-old youth leaders, and hack journalists who had passed themselves off as the Mainstream Right for the last generation, and they at once came to imagine that their occupation of office, their endless series of balls, soirees, roasts, and other posh social events dedicated to congratulating themselves, and their rapid abandonment of every significant political principle they had entoned for the last 20 or 30 years constituted "victory" and a "conservative revolution," no matter how many new government agencies were created or old ones preserved to give them the jobs, salaries, and social glamor they had always been denied in their much-ballyhooed private sector.

It was hardly surprising, therefore, that the apparatchiks of the Soft Right core of the Reagan administration at once forgot, if they had ever been cognizant of, the Middle American constituencies that had elected Mr. Reagan and made their fortunes for them, and for the remainder of the 1980s, Court Conservatives devoted themselves to figuring out how they could betray their Middle American base and, as they liked to put it, "lure" more blacks and Hispanics into Republican ranks and otherwise more credibly convince the archons of liberalism how harmless they were. The end result, of course, was the Kemp campaign of 1988, and it was hardly surprising that a candidate who sought to win the votes of a largely white, suburban, middle class party by telling its voters how he wanted to make the black and Hispanic underclass the focus of his party and his administration through larger and more expensive government programs received less than 5 percent in the primaries.

But not only were the Court Conservatives assimilated by the glitter offered by the incumbent elite of Washington. As the Reagan administration rumbled on, the main funding mechanisms of organized conservatism through direct mail began to wither. Contributors either concluded that with the Gipper in the Oval Office delivering nasty cracks about the Evil Empire every Saturday, civilization had been saved, or they found that the groups and personalities to whom they had once given money had either ceased to function or were transparently unable to accomplish what they had vowed to do — to end abortion, restore prayer in schools, regain the Panama Canal, crush labor unions, string up the commies, and clean the pursesnatchers and rapists off the streets. There may be a sucker born every minute, but sooner or later the supply has to run low if they don't get their money's worth. Unable to finance their dubious causes by continuing to lift the checks of widows and orphans, the Court Conservatives turned to the organized philanthropy of foundations and corporations, which had little use for a Middle American agenda and were happily married to the same set of managerial interests in preserving the leviathan state as the forces most conservatives had always claimed to oppose.

With the assimilation of the Mainstream Right in the Reagan administration and the disintegration of its main financial and political base, the Middle American constituency of the administration and of most of the right was decapitated and ceased to be represented, and the prospects for the emergence of what for lack of a better term may be called a Hard Right based on Middle American alienation dimmed. The constituency continued to exist, but its leaders either went out of business or left politics or were absorbed into the government-think tank-magazine digestive tract of the Soft Right-Reagan-Bush organism.

The success of the Soft Right, however, could be only temporary, because its success meant that the Middle American political constituency on which its occupation of office depended was being ignored, aside from politically expedient gestures such as the Willie Horton ads in 1988. Sooner or later, economic dislocations and the drift to the left of the Soft Right and the Reagan-Bush administrations, coupled with residual alienation on the part of Middle American forces, meant that a serious political movement representing their interests and aspirations would be possible.

The significance of the Buchanan movement, then, is not that it is simply one more crusade of the "conservative movement," a movement that has all but disappeared as a serious political force and a coherent intellectual identity, but that it has shown, contrary to what was commonly believed on both right and left, that a "Hard Right" remains politically possible, not merely as an intellectual irritation but as a political movement able to gather a nationwide coalition of voters, attract culturally significant support, and (in 1992) at least threaten a sitting president. Obviously, if that is all it remains, it will soon devolve into the same kind of political and ideological ghetto that the Court Conservatives were, and if it ever happened to win a national election, it would soon find itself swallowed by the same entrenched powers that gobbled the Reaganites.

But the main reason the Reaganites were so easily assimilated by the incumbent elites was not only the fundamental intellectual shallowness and lack of character of so many of their leaders but also the simple fact that they remained preoccupied with the formalities of political power and were blissfully oblivious to its cultural underpinnings. Whereas the Old Right of the 1960s prided itself on its cultural sophistication (which it confused with living and working in Manhattan and socializing with Manhattanite intellectual luminaries), the New Right of the 1970s and 1980s liked to boast of its pragmatism and its scorn for ideas, culture, and the intellectual classes that are at the center of every successful modern political movement. The anti-intellectualism of the New Right was a principal reason why it was unable to govern once it had won elections in the 1980s and why it was so easily absorbed by neo-conservative elements who never had any intention of pursuing any kind of authentic conservative agenda. Once in office, New Rightists found that they had no clear conception of what they were supposed to do or how to do it, and the only people around who purported to know were ex-liberals eager to creep back into the crevices of the state from which they had been momentarily exiled.

If the Buchanan movement or the Middle American Revolution or the New Nationalism or whatever it is going to call itself is to survive and develop as a serious force in American politics, it needs to do more than merely raise more money, build a national political organization, or expand its list of voters. It needs to create a counter-culture that can sustain its political leaders once they hold office and develop the cultural and intellectual underframe that legitimizes political efforts. It must construct its cultural base not on the metropolitan elites of the dominant culture but on emerging forces rooted in Middle American culture itself. It is exactly that kind of cultural permeation that sets the stage for successful political revolution as well as for any successful government, "revolutionary" or not. Instead of grabbing the shadow of political power and desperately hoping that the incumbent elites will be fooled into letting it have the substance of power, it creates and develops a social and political force independent of the dominant culture, and when that force is sufficiently mature, the snake will shed its skin. The new, emerging force will find the acquisition of formal political power and the winning of elections relatively easy as the old elite loses legitimacy and the new one not only acquires but also defines legitimacy.

For all the rhetoric about "populism" on both right and left for the last twenty years or so, revolutions never succeed simply because the "people" want them and issue a "mandate" for them to happen. No government ever falls, wrote Lenin, unless it is first "dropped" by the governing elite that holds it, and no government ever rises unless another elite is willing to pick it up and push it into place. The authentic populist revolt of 1992 that has surfaced in the campaigns of Mr. Duke, Mr. Perot, and Mr. Buchanan is the most powerful current in American politics today, but it will not succeed by virtue of its own momentum but only by finding leadership that is able and willing to carry it to enduring and meaningful power.

[August, 1992]

An Electorate of Sheep

E ven the weariest presidential campaign winds somewhere to the sea, and this month, as the ever dwindling number of American voters meanders into the voting booths, the sea is exactly where the political vessels in which the nation sails have wound up. Water, water everywhere, but not a drop to drink.

It is symptomatic of the disease of American democracy that one of the most frequently cited differences between the Republican and Democratic tickets this year consists not in what their respective candidates say they will do in the White House but rather in who they might appoint to the judicial branch of government. Mr. Clinton has suggested that New York Governor Mario Cuomo would be a good Supreme Court justice, while Mr. Bush has pointed with pride to his record of sending to the bench such paragons of juristic erudition as Clarence Thomas and David Souter. Granted there probably would be a significant difference in how the appointees of the two candidates would vote once on the court, but in a healthy representative government, courts ought to exercise so little power that appointments to them should not be political issues at all. Moreover, there ought to be many other and much more obvious differences between the candidates, the parties, and the policies they espouse than either they or their supporters have claimed, and citizens ought not to have to grunt and wheeze painfully in order to grasp them.

In an otherwise brilliant and moving speech to the Republican National Convention last summer, Pat Buchanan endorsed President Bush and offered such reasons as he could think of to support him. But to tell the truth, this was the weakest part of Mr. Buchanan's address; he was obliged to dwell on the president's commendable personal war record of some fifty years ago as opposed to the still mysterious conduct of Mr. Clinton when he was of draft age in the Vietnam era. The contrast in this respect between the two candidates may well indicate an important distinction of character between them, but it's really rather stretching to claim that the two men's performance or non-performance in two different kinds of wars offers a compelling reason for enthusiastic support of the former fighter pilot.

Then there is the issue of "family values," a phrase that at last begins to evoke merely headaches and nausea. It is quite true that for all the Democrats' efforts to co-opt that slogan, they remain unduly influenced by organized lobbies of homosexuals, abortionists, womanologists, and people like Mr. Clinton's wife who believe strengthening the family consists in facilitating litigation against parents on behalf of their children. Yet despite the fraudulence of the Democrats' adherence to the institution of the family, it is significant that they find it politically expedient to fake such adherence, just as it is equally significant that the Republicans, for the most part, also fake it in a different way. For all the repetition and regurgitation of the slogan of "family values" at the GOP convention last summer, only Mr. Buchanan mustered the sort of authentic rhetorical anger and moral conviction that are the appropriate responses to the Democrats' sly exaltation of perversion and their calculated support for the destruction of natural relationships between parent and child.

There are, then, at least superficial differences between the two major political parties and at least personal differences between their leaders, and the persistence of such differences will comfort those Americans who continue to think that the political system today still offers them a real choice. But the truth is that the differences between the parties are far outweighed by their similarities. Both parties are committed to further expansion of the role of the federal state in managing and regulating the economy as well as private social relationships and institutions. Mr. Bush in his own remarks at the convention chose to dwell explicitly and expansively on his accomplishments in supporting the enactment of such measures as the Disabilities Act, the civil rights act of 1991, the Clean Air Act, child care legislation, and hate crimes laws, and he and several other speakers boasted of his "educational choice" bill, which would in reality go far toward establishing federal control of private schools. With respect to the fundamental issue of "Big Government," then, there is little real difference between the two political parties, and both of them now routinely invoke egalitarian and universalist ideology as the legitimizing conceptual framework for enhanced state power.

Nor is there much difference with respect to foreign policy. Mr. Clinton, if anything, is even more committed an exponent of globalism and the "New World Order" than Mr. Bush. For a few weeks prior to the Republican convention last summer, Mr. Clinton found it expedient to urge U.S. military intervention in the Balkan civil war for what he called "humanitarian reasons," even though virtually all senior military officers and officials were attesting to the dangers and sheer impossibility of effective U.S. involvement, even if someone somewhere could discover a plausible national interest in intervening. It might be thought that, given Mr. Bush's constant belaboring of his own foreign affairs experience and claims to expertise and his apparent good sense in staying out of the Balkans, he would have made Mr. Clinton's amateurish bellicosity a major issue in the campaign. He hasn't, and his silence, like the dog that didn't bark in the Sherlock Holmes story, may suggest a clue. Perhaps Mr. Bush, if re-elected, really does plan to intervene in the Balkans himself. In any case, there is little important difference between the two parties on the major issue of the proper American role in world affairs in the post-Cold War era. Both support continued adaptation of U.S. sovereignty and independence to the fictitious "global economy;" both support the integration of the planet into transnational trade zones that accrue to the benefit of multinational corporations; both support continued high levels of foreign aid and the export of democracy; both support or at least refuse to do anything significant to halt continued cultural and demographic deracination through massive immigration; and both support an expanded role for the United Nations and other supranational organizations in determining, legitimizing, and intervening in the policies and practices of independent nations, including those of the United States.

What has occurred in the two major political parties, then, is what the apostles of Cold War containment policies always prophesied would occur between the United States and the Soviet Union: convergence. Each political party seeks to emulate the more successful rhetoric and ideologies of the other, and each knows full well that the real political conflict is not determined so much by serious discussion of political principle and policy as by merely the manipulation and management of "voter behavior." The trick by which electoral victory is won is not to persuade citizens to support one or another of the two parties so much as it is to hang on tightly to those blocs and clusters that, for reasons of habit and interest, constitute one's electoral base, while mounting media cavalry sorties into one's opponent's base with the hope of carrying away some of their maidens to one's own camp, where they will endure a fate worse than death. He who gets the most maidens while keeping his own wins the election.

It is all very well to blame the politicians, managers, media wizards, and incumbents who profit from this system, but the truth is that it is the citizens themselves who permit it to flourish and endure. It is a universal characteristic of modern mass organizations that they encourage dependency and passivity, that most of the individuals who are members of these organizations cannot possibly understand or acquire the highly technical skills that enable the organizations to exist and function, and that the role of most of their members is entirely passive and subordinate while power and responsibility is centered in an elite that does understand and perform their technical operations. Lacking any real power or responsibility, the members merely do their jobs and behave as they are told to behave. This is why you usually receive such terrible service in government offices and larger stores (it's not the clerks' store, and it makes little difference to them whether the customer is satisfied or not), why so few customers complain about it (they are told not to expect courtesy or help because the store is "self-service"), and also why television sitcoms have to play recorded laughter to let the mass audience know when something funny has been said or done (the members of the audience are also passive and will respond to whatever signal is sent to them). In mass politics, the role of "citizenship" is largely confined merely to passive voting for whichever of the two organizational monoliths the citizen has been enticed to support. Comparatively few citizens even do that today, and the number who hand out petitions or work for candidates or run for office themselves is a minuscule part of the population.

The result of this inculcation of passivity is that even populist revolts such as that of the Perot movement last spring and summer cannot survive apart from manipulation and managed leadership. Despite all the enthusiastic support Mr. Perot's phantom candidacy attracted, no sooner had he withdrawn from the race than the whole bubble popped, usually in tears and whining at the "cowardice" and "betrayal" of the leader, and the only question asked of his followers, the only question they seem to have asked themselves, was which of the other two candidates would they support. It never occurred to any of them to assert active leadership of the movement themselves and fill the void that the Texas billionaire had pretended to create and fill.

Indeed, the inculcation of passivity by the managerial system and its elite is an essential foundation of its power, not only on the political level but also on the social, economic, and cultural levels as well. The entire structure of the system depends upon manipulating its members into believing (or not challenging the assumption) that they are not capable of performing the simple social functions that every human society in history has performed as a matter of routine. It is the constant instruction of the propagandists of the system that we are not capable of educating our own children, taking care of them without brutalizing them, providing for our own health or old age, enforcing our own laws, defending our own homes and neighborhoods, or earning our own livings. We are not capable of thinking our own thoughts without ubiquitous and self-appointed pundits to explain to us what we see and hear nor of forming our own tastes and opinions without advice from experts nor even of deciding when to laugh when we watch television.

What is really amazing about American society today is not that there is so much violence and resistance to authority but that there is so little, that there is not or has not long since been a full-scale violent revolution in the country against the domination and exploitation of the mass of the population by its rulers. A people that once shot government officials because they taxed tea and stamps now receives the intrusions of the Internal Revenue Service politely; a society that once declared its independence on the grounds of states' rights now passively tolerates federal judges and civil servants who redraw the lines of electoral districts, decide where small children will go to school, let hardened criminals out of jail without punishment, and overturn local laws that are popularly passed and have long been enforced.

Is it any wonder that the two political parties and all their repulsive leaders, managers, speechwriters, image-makers, officials, fundraisers, vote-catchers, and candidates are frauds who are less convincing than street-corner card sharks? Why should they not be frauds? Who is there to expose their racket and hold them to account? "If God did not want them sheared," says the bandit leader in the movie "The Magnificent Seven" about the Mexican peasants he is robbing and killing, "he would not have made them sheep." The peasants in the movie prove they aren't sheep not by hiring the seven gunfighters to protect them but by finally taking up arms themselves. Sheep don't fight back; they wait for others to fight for them. If there remain today any Americans who are not sheep, they'll stop trying to hire phony populist gunfighters to save them from the wolfish bandits who run the country, and in the next four years they'll start learning how to shoot for themselves.

[November, 1992]

Gangbusters

In *The Killer Angels*, Michael Saara's novel about the battle of Gettysburg, there is a character named Col. Arthur Fremantle, a British military observer attached to the Confederate forces. In part a comic figure, Fremantle is perpetually perplexed by Americans in general and Southerners in particular, and he painfully worries himself and others with his seldom-very-acute perceptions. One thing he can't understand is why all the Southerners he meets are always so polite, and when he finally figures it out, he explains his discovery to Gen. Lewis Armistead, who later recounts it to his colleagues. "That Fremantle is kind of funny," says Armistead. "He said that we Southerners were the most polite people he'd ever met, but then he noticed we all of us carry guns all the time, wherever we went, and he figured that maybe that was why."

For once, Col. Fremantle may have hit upon an important truth, one that pertains not only to the antebellum South but also to human society in general. Armed societies are courteous societies, and many of history's most heavily armed social orders besides the Old South — those of the ancient Greeks, medieval European knights, Japanese Samurai, Renaissance courtiers, and barely literate cowboys on the American frontier — have also been noted for the elaborate rituals of courtesy and chivalry they practiced. The word "chivalry" itself, now a synonym for the old-fashioned style of deportment at which the emancipated strumpets of President Clinton's cabinet and household snort, derives from the code of the human battle tanks that rode horseback in the Middle Ages. The reason for the relationship between good weapons and common courtesy ought to be clear. With just about everyone you meet clanking a sword or packing a pistol, you'd better mind your manners, and your manners had better be highly formalized in clearly defined, normative patterns of conduct that leave no doubt about the benevolence of your intentions and the innocence of your behavior.

The converse also appears to be true. The society of late-twentieth century America is perhaps the first in human history when most grown men do not routinely bear arms on their persons and boys are not regularly raised from childhood to learn skill in the use of some kind of weapon, either for community or personal defense — club or spear, broadsword or longbow, flintlock or Bowie knife. Ours also happens to be one of the rudest and crudest societies in history, having jubilantly swept most of the etiquette of speech, table, dress, hospitality, regard for fairness, deference to authority, and the relations of male and female and child and elder under the fraying and filthy carpet of politically convenient illusions. With little fear of physical reprisal, Americans can be as loud, gross, disrespectful, pushy, and negligent as they please. Yet if more people carried rapiers at their belts or revolvers on their hips, it's a fair bet you'd be able to go to a movie and enjoy the dialogue from the screen without having to endure the small talk, family gossip, and assorted bodily noises that many theater audiences these days regularly emit.

The prospect of a society in which you can put a bullet between the eyes of drivers who grab a parking space for which you've been waiting or meet under the oaks at dawn characters who bray sexual and scatological slang in the hearing of your wife and children in restaurants will no doubt strike most Americans today as brutal, but the fact is that that is precisely how most societies in human history have disciplined themselves. For the most part, of course, bloodshed over such slights did not occur, because the slights themselves did not take place and most people knew the price they might have to pay for indulging in the ethic of Me First and What's Yours Is Negotiable. Today, discourtesy is commonplace precisely because there is no price to pay for it. Habitual rudeness is too trivial a disruption of the social bond for even the ubiquitous American megastate to notice or control, and if it becomes too unbearable for the dwindling number of Americans who are repelled by it to stomach, they simply avoid locations where they're likely to encounter it. They move to the suburbs, which they perhaps imagine are the last redoubts of safety and civility, places where they won't have to fight to defend themselves or the way of life they prefer and where they can rely on somebody else to fight for them.

But in the last year or so, there have been indications that even that escape fantasy is being denied to Middle Americans as criminals and their close predecessors on the evolutionary tree of incivility, just plain boors, pursue them beyond the city limits. Last summer in suburban Maryland, a woman who was driving her pre-school child to a day care center was kidnapped and murdered by two worthies from the District of Columbia. They pushed her out of her car and broke her neck and then pitched the baby out of the moving vehicle. This sort of crime is fairly common in the District itself, but the woman's neighbors in Howard County weren't used to it. "One of the things the real estate agent said," a neighbor told the *Washington Times* soon after, "was that Howard County has the lowest crime rate and that this area has the lowest rate of all." Virginian suburbanites expressed similar sentiments in the aftermath of the random killings by a wandering lunatic near CIA headquarters during the height of the rush hour earlier this year in upscale McLean, Virginia. "I moved out here to be safe," whimpered a local clergyman to the *Washington Post* the day after the shootings. "Now I can't even drive in the suburbs."

The emergence of routine rudeness and discourtesy and the eruption of serious crime in suburbs as well as cities are both part of the same pattern of social and civil decomposition that the United States is enduring, and the removal of force as a social control on both of them is perhaps the major underlying reason for their appearance. "Disguise it how you will," wrote the Victorian conservative theorist and lawyer Fitzjames Stephen, "it is force in one shape or another which determines the relations between human beings." Stephen regarded force as the foundation not only of law and government but also of social relationships, and he would have understood what is happening in the United States today as quickly and clearly as those police officers who have to live — and die — with it. Donald Murray, president of the Boston Police Protection Association, told the *Times* in the wake of the Maryland killing last year that "The criminal justice system has gone soft. Nobody has the guts to pull the lever on the electric chair. Instead, they tolerate increased violence, and every year the murder rate goes up."

Actually, Americans and even their lawmakers increasingly are beginning to rediscover the inverse relationship between the level of force available and social disorder, but unlike Stephen they persist in the delusion that force belongs only to and in the state and particularly in the federal government. Lawmakers understand the use of force at least to the degree that they know it's a good idea to pretend to support more of it as a means of controlling crime.

Thus, for the last couple of years a federal "crime control" bill has been bouncing around Congress that promises to inflict capital punishment for no less than 51 different offenses. By voting for it and bragging about it, the congressmen can boast to their constituents of how draconian they are on criminals, though when you examine the bill's provisions closely you will find that the crimes for which a convict can be hailed to the scaffold include such offenses as treason, espionage, and genocide. Death is a reasonable penalty for those who commit any or all of these, but executing those convicted of them does nothing to control the sorts of crimes most Americans have reason to fear. No one is really afraid of being mugged by Julius Rosenberg or raped in the parking lot by Pol Pot. In fact, most of the rest of the bill's sanguinary language merely protects federal bureaucrats and congressmen, not the ordinary citizen, by inflicting death on the killers of just about every professional political parasite from the visiting dignitaries of foreign countries to egg inspectors in the Department of Agriculture.

Whenever using more force as punishment or deterrent is discussed these days, it is almost always in terms of how to enhance the power of the mega-state itself and to strip average Americans of whatever means of force they have left to protect themselves; it never involves the removal of the political and legal restraints on the use of force by social authorities. Gun control and expanding the numbers of policemen, prosecutors, and prisons are among the favorite gimmicks advanced by what preens itself as the "tough on crooks" school, and of course our friends the neo-conservatives are in the forefront of peddling its doctrine. The original plans of "drug czar" Bill Bennett for the Bush administration's much ballyhooed "war on drugs" were the prototype for a veritably Napoleonic expansion of federal power that would have placed Mr. Bennett at the center of an iron web of national law enforcement, international diplomacy, the coordination of military forces, and the dispensation of billions of dollars to federal, local, and state police, educators, rehabilitators, and therapists. President Bush, perhaps sensing the implicit *coup d'etat* that the drug czar was trying to pull on him and the nation, wisely gutted most of it, and Mr. Bennett, his fun spoiled, eventually announced a tremendous but fictitious victory in the war on drugs and fled the administration a couple of years later.

But the drug czar's visions of a vastly expanded federal role in law enforcement live on in the neo-conservative mind. Last year, just after the Los Angeles riots, Terry Eastland, Mr. Bennett's one-time boon companion, mouthpiece, and ghost-writer, unbosomed himself of a brainstorm for further enlargement of federal crime control. Complaining that Lyndon Johnson's response to the Watts riots of 1965 hadn't included enough federal law enforcement, Mr. Eastland wrote that Johnson "believed law enforcement should remain a local matter. Conservatives have long believed that too, but Mr. Bush will also make a mistake if he rejects the need for a deeper federal law enforcement presence in the nation's inner cities." While neo-conservatives shudder at the word "nationalism" when it refers to an America First foreign policy and trade doctrine, they smack their lips with glee when the term can be drafted to bolster federal power and implement Big Government conservatism. "Nationalism must prevail when the most fundamental right of all — to self-preservation — can no longer be secured by local authorities," entoned Mr. Eastland.

Yet the lesson of the experience of the last sixty years or so of federal involvement in law enforcement is that there is far too much of it. Think, for a moment, of the federal agencies already engaged in police work: the FBI is the most obvious, but there is also the Drug Enforcement Administration, the Internal Revenue Service, the Immigration and Naturalization Service and the Border Patrol, the U.S. Marshals Service, the Secret Service, the U.S. Customs Service, the Bureau of Alcohol, Tobacco, and Firearms, the Bureau of Prisons, and the inspectors for the U.S. Postal Service, in addition to the whole apparatus of the military police and criminal investigation services of the armed forces, not to mention divers and sundry inter-agency task forces, federal prosecutors, judges, court officials of one kind or another, and the quietly enlarging role of the armed forces themselves and the CIA in enforcing the drug laws. Does anyone other than enthusiasts of reruns of *The Untouchables* imagine for a second that this labyrinth of bureaucracies has made American society any safer than it was before any of them existed?

Moreover, since the "incorporation doctrine" was foisted off on the legal system, the federal courts have presided over what is nothing less than a revolution in criminal law whereby every unsolicited confession of a street-corner grifter and every poke of a policeman's nightstick in the ribs of a pimp or a pusher yields yet another new revelation of a hitherto latent meaning of the Bill of Rights. By slyly reshaping the Constitution's limitations of federal power into restrictions on state and local authority, the courts have managed to wreck most of what remains of effective local law enforcement in the country and centralize and censor its common sense procedures. What the courts have been unable to reach with their legal fictions has been mopped up by affirmative action programs that mandate the hiring of unqualified minorities and women as policemen and prevent the promotion of qualified officers.

Nor does the strategy of the federalization (more properly, the nationalization) of law enforcement promise to stop in the new age of Mr. Clinton and his policy harem of Hillary, Zoe, Kimba, Donna, and/or Janet. It took the new president nearly the whole of the first month of his administration to locate an attorney general who both supported him and also was sufficiently square with the law to pass the scrutiny of the checkbouncers, secret-leakers, plagiarists, and woman-drowners on the Senate Judiciary Committee, and when he finally discovered the incumbent Ms. Reno, she at once announced that her first priority of business as the nation's top gangbuster would be the welfare of children. Mr. Clinton himself probably knows no more about law enforcement than any other public responsibility, and he probably cares about it even less than he does for those things he may know something about, but he too went through the charade of "tough on crooks" earlier this year when he vowed to push for the hiring (largely with federal funds) of yet another 100,000 policemen to put on the nation's streets even as he also promised to sign more federal handgun legislation.

That, in a nutshell, is the long-standing liberal-neo-conservative law enforcement strategy: disarm the citizens and swell the power of the federal leviathan. It has nothing to do with protecting Americans from criminals or punishing the criminals themselves, let alone with restoring to the communities and citizenry the force they naturally need and ought to have to protect themselves. It has everything to do with enhancing the power of those who can expect to gain from an enlarged but largely incompetent federal law enforcement apparat and making certain no one outside the federal mega-state and the professional police agencies that profit from it has any power at all. The nationalization of law enforcement, even when it claims to be "tough on crooks," is a fraud that converts local public authorities into vestigial organs of the mega-state and robs social institutions of the force that disciplines society.

From at least the days when Franklin Roosevelt's first Attorney General, Homer Cummings, barnstormed about the country stumping for what he variously called a "national police force," an "American Scotland Yard," a "super police force," and, on one occasion, a "Federal Army of Justice" to wage his "war on crime," the grand design of the architects of the managerial state has been to replace what they view as the "chaos" and "backwardness" of local and state police departments with the scientifically planned, humanely progressive, and fashionably therapeutic experimentation of law enforcement administered from the purportedly cleaner corridors of Washington. Cops who know their beats and keep the peace on them and sheriffs who can tell the difference between the local ne'er-do-wells and dangerous criminals are supposed to yield to over-educated young ladies with master's degrees in womanology.

But law enforcement, like most of the other social functions Washington claims to be able to perform better than anyone else, is really not a very complicated matter. Most societies in history have never had much of a problem with controlling criminals, and they've never needed science, or therapy, or special training and task forces, or centralized bureaucracies, or indeed very many cops, to deal properly and speedily with killers, thieves, and rapists. What they needed and what they had at hand that we do not have was precisely the force that "in one shape or another ... determines the relations between human beings" and the will to make use of it. If Americans really want to take back their streets, their cities, and their suburbs and teach some manners to the clods and crooks that are pushing them out of the theaters, parking lots, shopping malls, and restaurants, a little force and the will to use it are all they need to accomplish the task.

[May, 1993]

A Story of the Days to Come

Early in December of last year, while President-elect Clinton was trying to come up with a Cabinet that would "look more like America," the U.S. Census Bureau published a report that told us what America really looks like and what it will probably look like sixty years from now. Presumably, Mr. Clinton will have departed from the White House long before the prophecies of the bureau's professional beancounters come true, but not even the cabal of questionable millionaires, hatchet-faced fag hags, and trendy minorities selected by the new president to run the country for the next four years bears any resemblance to the rulers of the days to come or the population they will rule. Indeed, the subtext of the Census Bureau report suggests that within the lifetime of Americans now living, the United States as its citizens have known it for the last two centuries will, for all practical purposes, cease to exist.

The report, written by demographer Jennifer Cheeseman Day, concludes that the U.S. population will grow from its present 255 million to 383 million in 2050, but the expansion of total numbers is not the most interesting finding of the report. It also concludes that by 2050, the Hispanic part of the U.S. population will have grown from its present 24 million to 81 million, that the "Asian and Pacific Islander" portion will have risen from 9 million in 1992 to 41 million, that the black population is "projected to almost double from 32 million in

164

1992 to 62 million," and that "the non-Hispanic White share of
the U.S. population would steadily fall from 75 percent in 1992
... to 53 percent in 2050." While non-whites and Hispanics
will increase by some 120 million between 1992 and 2050, the
white population will swell by a mere 11 million in that period,
and by the middle of the next century whites would be on the
eve of becoming a minority in the United States. The report
finds that

> Although three-quarters of the population is non-Hispanic
> White in 1992, this group would contribute only 30 percent
> of the total population growth between 1992 and 2000, 21
> percent from 2000 to 2010, and 13 percent from 2010 to
> 2030. This group would contribute nothing to population
> growth after 2030 because the non-Hispanic group would
> be declining in size.

The report attributes these changes in the ethnic and racial
composition of the country to differences in the birth rates of
the various groups and also to the immigration rates. "Currently," it states, "about 66 percent of all births are non-Hispanic White. That percentage is expected to fall to 61 in 2000,
56 in 2010, 48 in 2030, and 42 in 2050. All other race and
ethnic groups would increase their share of births." As for
immigration, "the U.S. population in the year 2000 is projected to be 9 million (3 percent) larger than it would have been
if there had been no net immigration after July 1, 1991. The
equivalent figures for 2010, 2030, and 2050 are 21 million (7
percent), 49 million (14 percent), and 82 million (21 percent)."
By 2050, that is, the population of the country will, in the
words of the *New York Times* reporting on the Census Bureau
publication, "include 82 million people who arrived in this country after 1991 or who were born in the United States of parents
who did. This group of immigrants and their children will

account for 21 percent of the population."

The Bureau's conclusions differ from earlier reports it has published because this time it makes use of rather different assumptions from those it employed in the past. In earlier reports, the Bureau assumed that the total fertility rate would fall. But, "since the late 1980's, after a relatively stable 15-year trend of low fertility, there has been a dramatic rise in total fertility levels to almost 2.1 births per woman. Secondly, convergence of fertility among race and ethnic groups is no longer assumed. Historical data show that though fertility rates for different groups do experience similar effects, there is little evidence to assume that their fertility rates will eventually converge."

Earlier Census Bureau reports also assumed that immigration would decline due to the Immigration Reform and Control Act of 1986. "The last report," the new report states, "assumed the Immigration and Reform [*sic*] Act of 1986 (IRCA) would partially reduce undocumented [i.e., illegal] immigration." That, indeed, was a major purpose of the act, as its sponsors repeatedly assured us, but "in fact, there is no evidence of any reduction in the undocumented movement. In addition, the Immigration Act of 1990 allows more immigration. For these reasons, the future immigration assumptions for undocumented, legal and refugee immigrants were increased."

The meaning of all these numbers, percentages, and quotations should be clear. By 2050, a white person born in the United States in 1990 will be sixty years old and will be part of a minority in the country his or her forefathers founded. The racial and ethnic groups to which he belongs will be dwindling in numbers and in their percentage share of the population. Moreover, since the Census Bureau report uses the Office of Management and Budget definition of "white" as "a person having origins in any of the original peoples of Europe, North Africa, or the Middle East," its count of whites living in the United States now and in the future does not refer exclusively to European-descended elements of the population but includes also non-European, African, or Arabic strains that most white Americans have not historically considered to be white and with which they share little cultural kinship.

The conclusions of the Census Bureau beancounters are not entirely new. In 1982, demographers Leon Bouvier and Cary B. Davis reached similar results about the future population of the United States in a study distributed by the Center for Immigration Research and Education, but their monograph attracted little notice. A few years later, *Time* magazine published a cover story (April 9, 1990), which found that "By 2056, when someone born today will be 66 years old, the 'average' U.S. resident, as defined by Census statistics, will trace his or her descent to Africa, Asia, the Hispanic world, the Pacific Islands, Arabia — almost anywhere but white Europe." These studies, however, were not the official word of the American mega-state itself, which the new report of the Census Bureau is, but when the report was published last year, even though it made the front pages of the *Washington Post* and the *New York Times*, there appeared to be little reaction from anyone, especially whites, to the news that the historic core of the population of the United States was about to experience a revolution.

The absence of shock from whites themselves at their imminent demographic demotion is perhaps not all that surprising. A population, ethnic group, culture, or race that allows itself to be taxed without consent or understanding, runs off to fight wars for causes and against countries for reasons it can't explain, and tolerates the level of criminal lawlessness and political corruption that Americans have come to accept probably just doesn't much care whether it even exists or not, let alone whether it remains the core group of its nation and civilization. Moreover, so permeated are our minds with the fantasy that all cultures, races, and ethnic groups are the same, that a member of one group can as easily doff his culture and put on a new one as he can strip off a T-shirt, that most Americans who were aware of the impending demographic revolution probably didn't see why it made much difference.

Nevertheless, it does make a difference — probably more difference than any of the various political, economic, and social changes the United States has ever experienced, and those Americans who do care about their country and its civilization ought to start thinking very seriously about what they can do to stop the revolution from proceeding. As the figures of the Census Report imply, the principal cause of the demographic revolution is immigration and the differential in birth rates between non-white immigrants and white natives of the United States. The main thing Americans must do to preserve their civilization and the ethnic base on which it is founded is to stop immigration, especially from countries that do not share the ethnic and cultural heritage of the the historic core of the nation.

Even *Time* had the wit to understand that what it called in its 1990 cover story "the browning of America" "will alter everything in society, from politics and education to industry, values and culture." This, from a magazine notorious for its superficiality, betrays a good deal more common sense than the proclamation from xenophile and champion of unrestricted immigration Julian Simon only a week earlier in *Forbes* (April 2, 1990) that "The claim that our basic values, institutions, habits will be altered by immigrants from a different culture, and permanently altered, is pure hooey. ... At a time when barriers are falling down everywhere, even trade barriers, the only barrier that hasn't fallen is the barrier to immigration." It really doesn't require much imagination (though more than Mr.

Simon can muster) to understand that the importation of massive population fragments from radically different cultures will affect the receiving culture.

Indeed, in the last few years, the role of immigration in determining culture has been the subject of major historical scholarship. The most comprehensive is probably the work of historian David Hackett Fischer in his mammoth 1989 work, *Albion's Seed*, a thousand-page study of the role of four British subcultures on the formation of American civilization. Professor Fischer identifies some 24 "folkways" or "the normative structure[s] of values, customs and meanings that exist in any culture." In his view, folkways do "not rise from the unconscious even in a symbolic sense — though most people do many social things without reflecting very much about them. In the modern world a folkway is apt to be a cultural artifact — the conscious instrument of human will and purpose. Often (and increasingly today) it is also the deliberate contrivance of a cultural elite." The folkways Fischer enumerates include normative patterns that govern such settled ways of doing and thinking as habits of speech, building, sex, food, dress, sport, time, wealth, work, rank, order, power, and freedom, and no doubt he could have added others. The Puritans of East Anglia who settled New England brought with them from that region cultural habits and beliefs that were signficiantly different from those imported from the south and west of England to Virginia or from North Britain and its Celtic fringe to the Appalachian hills, and those patterns of beliefs that immigrated to North America in the 17th and 18th centuries have persisted, often unconsciously, ever since. Bertram Wyatt-Brown, Grady McWhiney, and Forrest McDonald, among other recent major historians, have also pointed to the role of the original British immigrants to North America as the source of enduring American cultural habits.

In *The Rise of Selfishness in America*, a little-noticed but major book published in 1991, jazz historian James Lincoln

Collier discusses the equally important contributions to an evolving American culture made by the European immigrants of the 19th century. Unlike the British immigrants of the previous era, he argues, the Irish, German, Jewish, and Southern and East European immigrants who came to this country in the 1800s had little attraction to the prevailing Victorian ethic that the prevalent Anglo-Saxon stock had imparted. "The immigrants, then," he writes,

> were bringing to the United States an array of habits, attitudes, and folkways that conflicted, at times dramatically, with the prevailing American patterns of thought and behavior. They were, in sum, resolutely anti-Victorian in almost every respect. They did not believe in discipline, punctuality, sobriety — the order and decency of the Victorian ethic. They wanted instead to live as expressively as they could. In what spare time they could snatch from their jobs and family obligations they wanted to drink, to dance, to gamble, to have fun. It is hardly surprising, therefore, that the people of the old stock were appalled by their behavior. It seemed to them that the newcomers were intent upon destroying the decent and orderly society that they of the old stock were trying so hard to build and maintain.

The result, in Collier's view, was that the new immigrants of the 19th century imparted to America their own cultural habits centered around "expressiveness" through their predominance in the new industries of popular culture — sports, movies, music, theater, journalism, mass entertainment, and the mass vices offered by organized crime under the control of new immigrant godfathers.

The conclusions of such scholarship as that of Fischer, Wyatt-Brown, McWhiney, McDonald, and Collier are perfectly consistent with common sense — that people carry their cultures in their heads and their hearts and do not leave it behind when they move. Immigration, therefore, affects culture, importing new habits and patterns of thought and behavior that often conflict with the old habits of the culture that receives immigrants, and the history of the political and social conflicts of European and American history can be told in terms of such struggles between clusters of customs and those who bear them. Moreover, cultural habits are not randomly distributed; they tend to follow ethnic and even racial lines, since most people acquire their cultural habits from their natural parents and families, if not from even more fundamental biological forces.

The demographic revolution that the Census Bureau predicts can therefore be expected to exert profound changes on American culture as it has flourished in our national history and as it exists now. The loss of political power by what the Census Bureau calls "non-Hispanic Whites" as they dwindle from a majority to a minority is only the most apparent such change, and it is hardly unreasonable to expect that what will follow from the transfer of power will be the outright dispossession and political and legal persecution of the white minority by a non-white and non-Western majority that has little experience of constitutional government, little respect for the rights of minorities and oppositional groups, and little love for whites or the West. Indeed, we already see the beginnings of that dispossession in affirmative action programs, hate crime laws, multiculturalist curricula, calculated insults to and vituperation of whites, and the proliferation of racially motivated atrocities against them. The demotion of "non-Hispanic Whites" as the demographic majority will almost certainly be accompanied by their demotion as the ethnic pool from which the American governing elite in political and economic life is drawn, and again we already see the beginnings of this form of dispossession too. Earlier this year the Knight-Ridder newspaper chain conducted a computer study of changes in the American workforce based on data drawn from the 1990 Census. It found, as *The Economist* (Jan. 9, 1993) reported, that "white men may soon be a minority of America's bosses. They are already a minority of the workforce. As recently as 1960, they held two-thirds of all jobs. Now they hold 45%." While the percentages of white males in American managerial positions have declined in the last decade, those of women, blacks, and Hispanics have risen in the same period. In March, the *Wall Street Journal* reported that U.S. corporations, ever indifferent to the health and survival of the culture, country, and people that enable them to function, are intent on hiring foreign professionals over their American counterparts. "Foreign professionals are becoming more attractive just as demand for some U.S. professionals, notably scientists and engineers, is at its lowest in at least a decade," the *Journal* reported. "The number of electrical engineers employed in the U.S. ... has fallen by one-fifth since its peak three years ago." Nearly every white male I know who has sought a professional position in the last few years has tales of blatant racial or sexual discrimination against him; in one case, a black employment official simply laughed at the applicant.

Yet while the demotion and dispossession of the groups that created, ruled, and sustained American civilization may effectively decapitate the civilization, the importation of non-Western habits of thought and behavior will very likely simply kill it outright. Not only the absence of a "folkway" of constitutional government but also the lack of a scientific and empirical tradition in non-Western societies, different concepts of work and time use, and different religious and ethical systems may well perpetuate within U.S. borders the political repression, violence, superstitions, filth, and apparent laziness of non-Western cultures. Parts of Florida, Texas, and southern California have already ceased to belong to the West in any but the administrative sense that they continue to pay taxes to Washington, and the same cultural meiosis is apparent in many major cities in other parts of the nation. Indeed, the very term "nation," derived from the Latin word for being born, will become meaningless when tens of millions are not born within the country's own borders.

Even as the Census Bureau published what may be the first lines of the epitaph of the American nation and its civilization last December, President Bush was plotting one last war in Somalia before he slipped into the twilight of history. The U.S. government, as George F. Kennan notes in his recent memoir, "while not loath to putting half a million armed troops into the Middle East to expel the armed Iraqis from Kuwait, confesses itself unable to defend its own southwestern border from illegal immigration by large numbers of people armed with nothing more formidable than a strong desire to get across it." Mr. Bush's last war and Mr. Kennan's latest reflections point to the central irony of the American imperium's last days, that the willingness of the American mega-state to kill some 250,000 Iraqis who had never harmed or threatened the United States in any way is regarded as the ultimate confirmation of the omnipotence of a superpower that has ended history and can now do whatever it wants, while the same power cannot imagine any good reason to protect its own borders from invasion. The mega-state and its masters can play with bombs in Baghdad and Bosnia all they want, save as many Somalis as can be rounded up, and count as many beans as they can find, but those enterprises will not preserve a civilization or a nation whose founding demographic core is facing a slow extinction and whose leaders have forgotten what civilization means and have come to regard their own nation as a barrier to be broken down and discarded.

[June, 1993]

Culture and Power
"Winning the Culture War"

Address to the American Cause Foundation
Washington, D.C., May 15, 1993

The first thing we have to learn about fighting and winning a culture war is that we are not fighting to "conserve" something; we are fighting to overthrow something. Obviously, we do want to conserve something also — our culture, our way of life, the set of institutions and beliefs that distinguish us as Americans and provide enduring norms by which we can judge our conduct. But we must understand clearly and firmly that the dominant authorities in the United States — in the federal government and often in state and local government as well, in the two major political parties, in big business, the major foundations, the media, the schools, the universities, and most of the system of organized culture, including the arts and entertainment — not only do nothing to conserve what most of us regard as our traditional way of life but actually seek its destruction or are indifferent to its survival. If our culture is going to be conserved, then, we need to dethrone the dominant authorities that threaten it.

Granted, we still have a democratic political system in which opposition and dissent remain in principle legal, but we all know the difficulty encountered by those who actually try to use their political and civil liberties to challenge the dominant authorities. Genuine dissent from the egalitarian, feminist, homophile, multiculturalist, and socialist agendas of the dominant authorities is seldom permitted in establishment media and often is outright punished, intimidated, or actually terrorized.

Nevertheless, there remain sufficient loopholes in the apparatus of power constructed by the dominant authorities in the United States to permit the organization of effective resistance to those agendas by democratic and legal means, if we have the will and the wit to use them. When I call for the overthrow of the dominant authorities that threaten our culture, then, I am not advocating illegal or undemocratic processes, but the war for the culture is nonetheless a radical or even a revolutionary conflict because it involves an almost total redistribution of power in American society — the displacement of the incumbent governing and cultural elites, the dismantlement of their apparatus of domination, the delegitimation of their political formulas and ideologies, and the radical decentralization of power and control of cultural norms from the hands of the present elite to those of the Americans who remain loyal to their traditional cultural and national identity.

Understanding that the main strategic goal of cultural traditionalists is the overthrow of the dominant authorities in the United States leads us into a somewhat anomalous position. Ever since its formal appearance in the late 18th century, conservatism has generally been associated with the defense of existing authorities, and its ideas as well as its rhetoric and its basic psychology have historically been designed to conserve, not to challenge or overthrow. Hence, while we will find much in the conservative tradition to teach us about the nature of what we want to conserve and why we should want to conserve it, we will find little in conservative theory to instruct us in the strategy and tactics of challenging dominant authorities. Instead, we need to look to the left to understand how a politically subordinated and culturally dispossessed majority of Americans can recover its rightful position as the dominant and creative core of American society.

By far the most relevant figure on the left in the 20th century for this purpose is the Italian communist theorist Antonio Gramsci, whose idea of "cultural hegemony" has directly or indirectly facilitated the cultural revolution that the enemies of American civilization have pulled off in the last half century. I do not claim that Gramsci's ideas were consciously followed by those who seized cultural power in the United States — indeed, the beginnings of the cultural revolution of the left long predated Gramsci's influence — but it is true that the process by which that revolution occurred resembled the strategic and tactical ideas that Gramsci later articulated, and it is probably the case that most successful revolutionaries possess an instinctive understanding of these ideas and know how to apply them. If the cultural right in the United States is to take back its culture from those who have usurped it, it will find a study of Gramsci's ideas rewarding.

Gramsci lived from 1891 to 1937, and in the aftermath of World War I he played a major role in the founding of the Italian Communist Party and worked with the Comintern. He was arrested by the Fascists in 1926 and was imprisoned from that year until 1934, by which time he had contracted tuberculosis. He was released from prison and, his health broken by his imprisonment, died in 1937 at the age of 46. Most of his writing he did in prison in the form of what are now known as the "Prison Notebooks," which are often disjointed and opaque in style and structure, as might be expected of books written in one of Mussolini's jails.

What distinguishes Gramsci's Marxism from that of most of his predecessors and contemporary Marxists is that while most of them, following Lenin, emphasized the need to capture and control the state, Gramsci argued that this was not the appropriate tactic in Western Europe or the United States. In those societies, the capitalist class, he argued, had succeeded in manufacturing what Gramsci called "ideological hegemony" by control of the cultural institutions of society — religion, education, the arts, the very processes of thought, taste, and emotion. While as a Marxist Gramsci believed this kind of hegemony was no less repressive than the economic and political repression Marx and Lenin had discussed, he also understood that the "masses" or working classes had essentially internalized the ideological formulas, myths, values, and norms that this ideological hegemony imposed, so that actual reliance on force by the ruling class was largely unnecessary.

The main implication of the cultural or ideological hegemony of the capitalists in Europe and America, in Gramsci's view, was that the strategy of revolution there had to be different from what it had been in Russia. While in Russia capturing the highly centralized czarist state was the key to a successful revolution, in the West the ruling class only partially depended on the state. "In the East," Gramsci wrote, "the state was everything, civil society was primordial and gelatinous; in the West, there was a proper relation between state and civil society, and when the state trembled a sturdy structure of civil society was at once revealed. The state [in the West] was only an outer ditch, behind which there stood a powerful system of fortresses and earthworks."

In other words, overthrowing the state or capturing it would do the revolutionary little good, since the real power of the old ruling class rested on its cultural hegemony, and if the revolution were to succeed, it would have to challenge the cultural hegemony of the ruling class even more than it challenged its political hegemony. "A social group," he wrote, "can, and indeed must, already exercise '[moral and intellectual] leadership' [i.e., cultural hegemony] even before winning governmental power (this indeed is one of the principal conditions for the winning of such power); it subsequently becomes dominant when it exercises power, but even if it holds it firmly in its grasp, it must continue to 'lead' as well."

It does no good for revolutionaries to come to power simply through control of the coercive apparatus of the state if the masses they intend to rule still retain the internalized beliefs instilled in them by the ruling class, since the result would be merely reliance on force by the revolutionaries and the kind of total state repression that emerged in Russia under Lenin and Stalin. What the revolutionary must do, then, is to seize cultural power before the seizure of political power.

How this seizure of cultural power can be accomplished was the subject of a good deal of Gramsci's own political work as a communist organizer before his imprisonment and of much of his writing while in prison. Essentially, he argued that instead of relying on the bureaucratized and elitist party structure that Lenin had built, revolutionaries must build what he called a "counter-hegemonic force" that would flourish parallel to but independent of the social and cultural institutions under the control of the ruling class and which would challenge the authority of the ruling class, its values and norms, while constructing its own authority in accordance with socialism. As Carl Boggs, a Marxist commentator on Gramsci, writes, "Not only must the old meanings and norms of everyday life be destroyed, but new ones must be constructed in their place. Hence, the struggle for ideological hegemony has two phases: to penetrate the false world of established appearances rooted in the dominant belief systems and to create an entirely new universe of ideas and values that would provide the basis for human liberation."

Gramsci's specific idea for building this counter-hegemonic force in Italy was to work with "workers' councils" that were set up in the industrialized cities of northern Italy after World War I, and these councils, similar to the Russian soviets that had existed in the early days of the Bolshevik revolution, would gradually take over both the economic and political functions of Italian capitalism and the state as well as generate a new mass consciousness that would assert cultural hegemony in place of that of capitalist society. In the event, this application of Gramsci's ideas did not work, because the workers' councils were ruthlessly suppressed, both by the Italian government after World War I as well as by the Fascists once they had seized power.

What is important to understand about Gramsci's strategy of cultural hegemony, however, is, first, that it recognizes that political power is ultimately dependent on cultural power — that human beings obey because they share, perhaps unconsciously, many of the assumptions, values, and goals of those who are giving them orders and that without these shared assumptions, power must depend entirely on force — and, second, that in order to challenge the dominance of any established authority, it is necessary to construct a countervailing cultural establishment, a "counter-hegemony" or, as the New Left of the 1960s called it, a "counter-culture," that is independent of the dominant cultural apparatus, does not share its assumptions, values, and goals, and is able to generate its own system of beliefs and ideas as an alternative to that of the ruling class.

As I indicated earlier, these concepts were not entirely new, and they had been applied, probably instinctively, by the Progressivists, Marxists, liberals, and others on the left in the United States throughout the first part of the 20th century as the left gradually established its dominance in the mass media, the foundations, the universities, and the federal state. That dominance has intensified in recent years as veterans of the New Left, often directly influenced by Gramsci, have occupied strategic positions in such institutions and have used them to construct the cultural hegemony that we know as "political correctness." In the case of the American left, because it has so totally lacked any popular support at the grassroots level, it has been unable to build the kind of independent counter-cultural institutions that Gramsci wanted and has had to rely on the infiltration and permeation of established institutions, and especially on governmental power.

Moreover, the left has not been the only group to apply this strategy. It is interesting to note that Adolf Hitler seems to have conceived much the same idea in the aftermath of his failed coup d'etat in the 1924 Beer Hall putsch. Speaking to a group of veterans of the putsch in November, 1936, after he had come to power, Hitler remarked that "We recognized that it is not enough to overthrow the old State, but that the new State must previously have been built up and be practically ready to one's hand. ... In 1933 it was no longer a question of overthrowing a state by an act of violence; meanwhile the new State had been built up and all that there remained to do was to destroy the last remnants of the old State — and that took but a few hours."

William L. Shirer shows how in the years between the failed putsch of 1924 and Hitler's coming to power in 1933, he and the Nazis built up an entire series of party institutions that paralleled and duplicated those of the existing state, including groups for women, youth, workers, students, artists and intellectuals, as well as the party's propaganda organs and its paramilitary forces, so that by the time Hitler won the 1933 election, the national socialist state had already been "prefigured" (to use a term of Gramsci) in the party organization, and the

actual seizure of state power merely enabled the party to sub-
stitute its own apparatus for that of the old state.

The strategy that both Hitler and Gramsci were devising
was essentially to construct what historian Crane Brinton in his
classic *Anatomy of Revolution* called an "illegal government"
parallel to and independent of the existing legal government.
"The legal government," wrote Brinton, "finds opposed to it,
not merely hostile individuals and parties ... but a rival government, better organized, better staffed, better obeyed. ... At a
given revolutionary crisis they step naturally and easily into the
place of the defeated government."

In Gramsci's term, the rival government or "counter-hegemonic force" "prefigures" the post-revolutionary state by
duplicating and eventually taking over the functions of the pre-
revolutionary state. The construction of such a parallel or rival
government has been characteristic of all the revolutions of
modern history, including the American revolution.

While Gramsci and Hitler sought to develop their cultural
strategy for totalitarian ends, communist in the case of Gramsci
and national socialist in the case of Hitler, the same strategy
can be used for conservative purposes, and probably even more
successfully in the United States since beneath the encrustation
of the dominant cultural apparatus of the left in this country
there still persists an enduring cultural core of traditional beliefs and institutions. Indeed, while the American right has
generally ignored cultural forces, preferring to dwell on economic, foreign policy, and narrow political issues and to concentrate on policy bargaining within the government (and usually on the terms defined by their opponents), the European
New Right explicitly invokes Gramsci as a source of its ideas
and strategy. Thus Tomislav Sunic writes in his account of the
European New Right,

The real force that sustains liberalism and socialism is the cultural consensus which reigns more or less undisturbed in the higher echelons of education and legal systems. Once these cultural centers of power are removed, the system must change its infrastructure. ... The main reason that conservative movements and regimes have been unable to gain lasting political legitimacy lies in their inability of successfully infiltrating the cultural society and introducing another "counter-ideology" to the masses. Should conservative movements genuinely desire to become politically consolidated, they must first and foremost elaborate their own cultural strategy, which will ultimately help them to dislodge socialist and liberal leverage on the political arena. One must first conquer the brains before conquering the state.

The inadequacy of the political power of the right in America in the absence of cultural power is perfectly illustrated in the cases of the Nixon, Reagan, and Bush administrations. None of the Republican administrations possessed sufficient cultural resources and allies to enable whatever ideas and policy initiatives they expressed to endure, and much of their time and energy were consumed with quibbling over, explaining, and often retreating from what they put forward in the face of the almost total opposition of the dominant cultural elite in the mass media and the higher circles of education. The Republicans had indeed won election to the "outer ditch" of government, but none of them ever came close to penetrating the "powerful system of fortresses and earthworks" of cultural hegemony on which the real power of the left rests. The Bush administration in particular came to rely on an essentially liberal framework of discourse to justify its actions. As a result, far more important than the eventual political defeat of Republican office-holders, the administration accomplished almost nothing in altering the framework of public discussion or to challenge the fundamental terms of debate in American political culture, so that today it is far more difficult to argue publicly against the legitimacy of homosexuality, against affirmative action, against the welfare state and its assumptions about man and government, or against a globalist foreign policy than it was before Bush, Quayle, Kemp, and William Bennett gave us the benefit of their wisdom. By replicating and repeating the rhetoric of the left, the American right merely confirms and legitimizes the cultural dominance — and therefore the political power — of the left.

Nor does there seem to be much prospect that the Republican Party as it is now constituted will offer any serious challenge to that cultural dominance, or that the tame neo-conservative intelligentsia that serves as the GOP's ideological vanguard will do so. Thus, neo-conservative Michael Joyce, president of the $420-million Bradley Foundation of Milwaukee, which the *National Journal* calls "the nation's largest underwriter of conservative intellectual activity," recently told the *Journal* that "I'm ... not ready to repeal the welfare state. I want to ameliorate the problems of the welfare state." Similarly, last spring, just after President Bush, under pressure from Pat Buchanan, fired NEA chairman John Frohnmayer, there began to build for the first time a small consensus even among some liberals that the NEA might not be necessary after all. Who should jump out of the woodwork to tell us that "abolitionist sentiment, however understandable and defensible, will be ineffectual" but Mr. Joyce's mentor, Irving Kristol, the ubiquitous godfather of the neo-conservatives, and it was Kristol's contribution to the *Kulturkampf* to suggest that all we really needed to do was just hand over the NEA to some neo-con manager who could fork up the pasta to the right people, namely the neo-cons.

More recently, Mr. Kristol has sallied forward to tell us, in the *Wall Street Journal* last December, that "I regret to inform Pat Buchanan that those [the culture] wars are over, and the left has won. ... the left today completely dominates the educational system, the entertainment industry, the universities, the media. One of these days the tide will turn," he writes, but there's nothing anyone can do about it now. Well, no doubt some day the tide will turn, but when it does it won't be because Mr. Kristol was paddling in the right direction. If Antonio Gramsci had had comrades like Irving Kristol and Michael Joyce, Mussolini could have used his prisons for more serious threats to his power.

As far as I can see, there is virtually no reason to think that either the Republican Party establishment or the neo-conservative intelligentsia or for that matter most of the mainstream conservative establishment either wants or is able to mount an effective challenge to the dominant cultural apparatus of the left in this country. They do not want to do so because they are perfectly happy holding petty offices, publishing reams of background papers, and giving each other immense financial donations within the left's framework of cultural and political hegemony, and the most that they want to do is trim up that framework, reform it, take it over themselves, and in Mr. Joyce's term, "ameliorate" it. They are not able to mount an effective challenge because the establishment right has long isolated itself from the grassroots foundations of the real American culture and locked itself in its phone booth, where they employ their time and money making conference calls to each other, periodically emerging to raid the direct mail icebox and venturing all the way to Milwaukee to squeeze another large slice of the Bradley family's fortune out of Mr. Joyce.

The people who are challenging the cultural hegemony of the left and are trying to construct a "counter-hegemonic force" are the American people themselves, through the efforts of leaders like Mary Cummins and her allies in the belly of the beast,

New York City, and through similar efforts, some of them represented at this conference today, in Colorado, Oregon, California, and other states where the long silent and dormant core of American civilization is beginning to awaken. These efforts are not the products of strategies thought out in the Beltway, and as far as I know they owe nothing to the financial largesse of conservative foundations. They are largely local in orientation and thereby reflect the authentic grassroots nature of the real American culture. They are independent of both the federal state as well as of the tentacles of its cultural extensions, so that they do not merely replicate and repeat the assumptions and values of the incumbent cultural regime and are able to express their own vision of culture, and in their activism they defy and challenge the kind of passivity that the dominant culture seeks to induce in Americans. If they are going to develop and flourish in the future, they need to undertake three things.

First, they need to expand and enlarge their numbers and adherents and avoid remaining in the political and cultural ghetto that so-called "movement conservatism" represents. This means that they cannot look to large conservative foundations or even to very many other conservatives for help, since the effect if not the purpose of those organizations is to make grassroots groups dependent on their assistance and thereby confine them within the ghetto. Grassroots groups need to find ways they can expand beyond those already sympathetic to them and enlist the energies of other Americans who have not previously been involved or interested in the waging of cultural war, and to do this they need to look for new issues beyond their present range of concerns and interests. By doing so not only will they gain strength through new adherents but also they will be able to retain their financial and organizational independence and the integrity of their agendas.

Second, these groups need, to use a phrase of the left, to raise consciousness — not only to expand their numbers but also to educate other Americans in how the Middle American core is exploited by the dominant authorities, how traditional American culture is being subverted and destroyed, and what this destruction means to the country and its citizens. Long-standing issues of the populist right like abortion or relatively new ones like homosexuality, school curricula, and gun control cannot be seen or fought in isolation from issues that have not previously been issues at all such as trade, immigration, and an America First foreign policy, and activists should use all these issues to inform previously inactive citizens and groups of how they are all the victims of an alien domination and of what they can do about it to resist it.

Third, grassroots efforts will eventually need to develop a national political consciousness and a national reach. While Gramsci was undoubtedly right that political power without cultural hegemony is pointless, it is these very grassroots groups that for the first time in living memory offer a firm cultural and popularly based foundation for enduring and effective political power on the right. Only if they can eventually be coordinated into a national movement that still retains its independence, its integrity, and its local and activist character can they become the effective political base for a national political campaign or a presidential administration, and only if a national campaign or an administration possesses such a national cultural base, can it or its supporters expect to accomplish what is necessary — to break the federal leviathan apart at its joints and dismantle its apparatus of cultural domination, its revolting and repressive culture, and its phony and disgusting cultural elite and to create a new national and cultural consciousness of what it means to be an American. The strategy by which this new American revolution can come to pass may well come from what was cooked up in the brain of a dying communist theoretician in a Fascist jail cell 60 years ago, but we can make use of it not to build the lies of socialism and the enslavement of communism but to conserve the freedom and dignity that American civilization has always represented and can represent again, if only we have the strength and the will and the common purpose to take back our country and our culture.

[December, 1993]

A Banner with a Strange Device

As the House of Representatives slithered toward its vote on the North American Free Trade Agreement last November, the regiments of lobbyists who were peddling the pact set up their tents in what the *New York Times* described as "a stately conference room on the first floor of the Capitol, barely an elevator ride away from the action in the House chamber." There, in the high-tech opulence with which the public interest is bought and sold, the real rulers of the United States bargained and bickered over the economic future and national sovereignty of the country. According to the *Times'* account of the scene, the "stately conference room" was plastered with banners that proclaimed the ethic of the New World hog trough into which the lobbyists were bartering the nation and which were intended to inspire those who required inspiration with a firm moral grounding for the bribery and lies by which they earn their bread. One of the banners tells us all we need to know about both NAFTA and the larger issues that stood on the auction block that week. "We Defend," it blared, "and We Build a Way of Life Not For America Alone, But For All Mankind." There was a time not too long ago when such banalities of humanitarian universalism were left to gather cosmic dust on the surface of the moon, but today they are taken seriously as formulas by which the managed evanescence of the United States is rationalized.

But for all the banality of the banner, the device it bore communicated an important truth about NAFTA and the forces that pushed it. Strangely enough, it was NAFTA opponent Jesse Jackson who perhaps encapsulated those forces most succinctly in a statement uttered soon after the vote. "President Clinton," the country's most voluble Professional Negro proclaimed, "leads the Reagan-Bush-Limbaugh-Iacocca-Kissinger-Rostenkowski-major publishers-Wall Street-Republicans victory team." While this, of course, is not a precise analysis, the Rev. Jackson's proclamations are never noticeable for their precision or their analytic clarity, but at least this one doesn't rhyme. Nevertheless, his description does accurately suggest that it was the nation's elite that offered the most fervent apologetic for NAFTA, and not merely the corporate elite but also our political and cultural oligarchs. That is why Mr. Clinton could trot out every living ex-president in support of the treaty as well as the recently retired chairman of the Joint Chiefs of Staff and most of the country's governors, and that is why NAFTA lobbyists enjoyed such posh headquarters in the U.S. Capitol, while their opponents had to make do with rather less up-scale offices considerably farther from the elevators.

What binds these different elites together, however, is not merely their commitment to NAFTA but their larger investment in the emergent transnational regime, variously known as the "New World Order," the "Global Economy," the "First Universal Nation," etc., toward the construction of which, as Henry Kissinger announced, NAFTA is the first vital step. Probably more than any other political issue for years, NAFTA shows clearly the immense gulf that separates the interests of these elites from the interests and aspirations of Middle Americans. In an analysis of the NAFTA conflict soon after the vote, *Washington Post* reporter Thomas Edsall made it clear that the real source of the struggle over the trade agreement was not simply "left" versus "right" or "free trade" versus "protection" but rather a social conflict between the elite as characterized by Mr. Jackson and what Mr. Edsall described as "men and women without college degrees for whom the work ethic no longer is paying off. For the past 20 years, for men especially, their inflation-adjusted wages have been eroding, and the likelihood of permanent layoff has grown."

Democratic Whip David Bonior, one of the leading opponents of the trade agreement in the House, was even more specific about the Middle American opposition to the treaty. "When jobs are lost," he said in the debate on the House floor, "these are the people who have to sell their homes, pull their kids out of school and look for new work. The working people who stand against this treaty don't have degrees from Harvard. They don't study economic models. And most of them never heard of Adam Smith. But they know when the deck is stacked against them." It will be recalled, and Mr. Edsall did recall it, that it was precisely this stratum of the American population to whom Mr. Clinton pledged his troth in his acceptance speech at the Democratic Convention in 1992, "the people who work hard, pay their taxes, [and] play by the rules," and of course, as with every other successful presidential candidate who has gulled Middle Americans into supporting him, Mr. Clinton's practice in office has been to betray them at every opportunity and to ally himself with the elite and its interests.

The conflict between, on the one hand, the Middle American core of the American nation and, on the other, an elite lodged in the bureaucratized, technocratic, and increasingly global mass organizations of the state, economy, and culture is of course not new and has underlain and informed most of the social and political conflicts in the United States since the 1960s. Yet with the NAFTA debate the conflict reached a new level, turned a corner, and took a giant step toward an explicitly nationalist (and, on the other side, an explicitly anti-nationalist and globalist) consciousness. While earlier stages of the conflict have settled on cultural, racial, and social issues, what the NAFTA battle accomplished for the first time was to bind together and synthesize the economic complaints of the Middle American core with the issue of nationhood itself.

The opposition to NAFTA generally emphasized two major flaws of the agreement. One was its effect on American jobs and the "giant sucking sound" the agreement would cause the economy to emit as American jobs gurgled across the Rio Grande. The other was its erosive effect on national sovereignty through the trinational panels that the agreement empowers to rule on which local and state laws remain valid under the agreement's terms, thereby severely limiting American sovereignty, the degree to which Americans may make, enforce, or repeal the laws under which they live and work. Both are essentially nationalist issues, the latter concerning sovereignty obviously so but the former concerning the national economy no less so. It was the unique accomplishment of the best known opponent of the agreement, Ross Perot, to muff his implicit grasp of these nationalist issues in his disastrous debate with Vice President Gore just before the vote. By his useless chatter about the environmental depredations of American corporations in Mexico, Mr. Perot dropped the nationalist ball and succeeded only in showing that he didn't understand his own argument, which originally spoke to the effects of the agreement on his own country and its people.

Yet despite Mr. Perot's fumbling, NAFTA remained for

most of its opponents a nationalist issue, and the conjunction
of the Middle American economic crisis with the matter of
sovereignty for the first time in the NAFTA controversy raises
the level of the Middle American conflict by a notch or two.
Sovereignty, of course, has been an issue at the heart of
U.S. foreign involvement in the Gulf War, the Balkans, and
Somalia under United Nations authority for some years, but
for most Americans it has been a rather abstract and elusive
concern. Only when President Clinton actually transferred
military command of U.S. troops to foreign officers under
U.N. authority last year and only when body bags began to
come back to the United States from Somalia was the issue
of national sovereignty in the continuing adventures of New
World globalism rendered concrete. The NAFTA debate
rendered sovereignty not only concrete but also made it a
matter of dollars and cents, because it at once became clear
that the managed erosion and violation of national sovereignty that NAFTA enshrines were closely linked to the loss
of American jobs and the economic ruination of the middle
class. It suddenly dawned on millions of Middle Americans
that the diminution of national sovereignty would march in
step with the decline of their own economic position. Finally, NAFTA also made clear that if the material interests
of Middle Americans were linked to national sovereignty,
they were at odds with the interests of the transnational managerial elite, just as the interests of the elite also are closely
linked to the abandonment of sovereignty.

What NAFTA showed, then, was that two socio-political blocs have now emerged in American politics. On the
one hand, there is a Middle American core that remains not
only culturally and emotionally loyal to the institutions of
American nationality but also is materially interested in a
strong, independent, and sovereign nation and accurately sees

its material interests as in conflict with those of the dominant elites in the American economy, state, and culture. On the other hand, there is an elite driven by its multinational corporate and commercial interests to dilute, erode, and compromise the sovereignty of the American nation and at the same time and for the same material reasons to weaken the economic position of Middle America. The latter is not merely a side-effect but a deliberate strategy on behalf of the corporate structures the elite controls. In a column here last year, I quoted the remark of Donald V. Fites, chairman of the Caterpillar Corporation, to the effect that "there is a narrowing of the gap between the average American's income and that of the Mexicans. As a human being, I think what is going on is positive. I don't think it is realistic for 250 million Americans to control so much of the world's GNP." The jury may still be out as to whether Mr. Fites is really a human being, though it's pretty clear he's not much of an American, but his view is not exceptional among other "American" corporate leaders. "For the first time," the *New York Times* reported as long ago as 1987, "American manufacturers are talking openly about a new and startling wage goal: They want to greatly narrow the gap between what they pay their factory workers and the earnings of workers in South Korea, Brazil, and a handful of other third world countries." Robert E. Mercer, chairman of Goodyear, echoes this sentiment. "In one way or another," he vows, "the gap will have to close."

The reason the gap will have to close is intimately connected to the economic logic of world trade; U.S. firms cannot afford to pass up the bonanza of foreign markets, but they find themselves priced out of those markets by goods produced by the cheap labor of the Third World. They cannot swallow the rock of trade protectionism, by which the wage level of their American employees could be salvaged, since that would provoke retaliations by foreign nations that could close off access to world markets; but neither can they keep sitting in the uncompetitive hard place where the payment of high American wages puts them. Hence, something has to give, and of course what the corporate elite is eager to give is the economic position of Middle America, which the corporate managers have decided to convert into a Third World work force.

Hence NAFTA, which will achieve this goal in part by simply moving jobs to the Third World and in part by using the threat of movement as a club with which to hammer wage negotiations into acceptable shape. Hence also mass immigration, which imports a cheap work force in competition with American workers as well as a new urban underclass with which the governmental managerial elite can play its social-therapeutic games for a generation or more. As long as the interests of the managerial elites of corporate capitalism and the mega-state are placed ahead of those of the core of the American nation, this conflict between the interests of the elite and those of the Middle American core will persist, and only the displacement of the elite in both the corporate economy and the mega-state and of its structural interests in the organizations of Leviathan Capitalism and the Leviathan State can resolve the conflict in favor of Middle Americans.

Decades ago, Joseph Schumpeter showed how modern managerial capitalism subverts the very cultural fabric that produces it, and last August, in an article in *Harper's*, David Rieff showed how the real engine of the much-lamented "multiculturalism" that now subverts Western and American civilization in the nation's schools and universities is driven by what he called "Multiculturalism's Silent Partner," the "Global Economy."

The more one reads in academic multiculturalist journals and in business publications, and the more one contrasts the speeches of CEOs and the speeches of noted multiculturalist academics, the more one is struck by the similarities in the way they view the world. Far from standing in implacable intellectual opposition to each other, both groups see the same racial and gender transformations in the demographic makeup of the United States and of the American workforce. That non-white workers will be the key to the 21st century American labor market is a given in most sensible long-range corporate plans.

Mr. Rieff's article and the remarks of American corporate leaders quoted above point toward another social and political convergence that parallels that of the Middle Americans of the anti-NAFTA movement last fall. So far from constituting a culturally conservative force that works for the preservation of the nation and its demographic cultural core, the managerial regime and its elite in state, economy, and culture are the enemies of the nation and its people; managerial capitalism works to undermine, weaken, and destroy them, and therefore an alliance of managerial capitalism with the multicultural and anti-national left is natural and logical. And if that alliance also includes the Clinton administration as well as the globalist conservatism of Newt Gingrich, Jack Kemp, Ronald Reagan, Bob Dole, and Phil Gramm, it makes equal sense for the Middle American foes of NAFTA to make their bed with a nationalist right that places little faith in the Republican Party and its tepid ideologies but constructs a new political force founded on putting the interests of the American nation and the American people first. Last fall, these new alliances began to emerge and to engage in the struggle for the nation that their interests and aspirations compel. If the banners they waved then

seemed to bear strange devices, it may not be too long before the armies that march under them reshape American
politics on explicitly nationalist lines that the rest of the world
now finds familiar.

[February, 1994]

Global Retch

Nearly four years after George Bush, on the eve of the Persian Gulf War, first popularized the expression "New World Order," is there anyone in the United States who does not greet that phrase with either a grin of sarcasm or a growl of hatred? The answer, in a nutshell, is yes. The expression may have become a cliché and the concept may have stumbled and tripped far more than its conceivers anticipated, but what it expresses remains the main driving force in American foreign policy and in the minds that inhabit those cryptic circles where the course and contours of foreign policy are crafted.

The Gulf War, as a number of its critics pointed out at the time, was merely an experiment, a vanguard action intended to test the waters and see how far the trappings of patriotism and the jolliness that always accompanies successful military slaughter could be exploited to mobilize the American populace for the higher purpose of global salvation. The answer to the question "how far?" turned out to be "very far," and the national chest-thump that celebrated the mass murder of some 250,000 Iraqis who never even contemplated attacking Americans suggested that the architects of the global cow pasture could easily recruit all the sit-com-saturated cattle they needed to serve in future round-ups.

Since the end of the Gulf War, however, the embryonic global regime those architects planned to construct has not slouched forward to be born. Stage Two of its birthpangs was supposed to take place in the Balkans, but not even the architects could delude themselves that the Balkan terrain and politico-military conflict lent themselves to the kind of high-tech juggernaut that Mesopotamia permitted. In lieu of a Balkan crusade, we had to make do with the dunderheaded mission in Somalia, and that, with all its prospects of tossing lollipops to starving children while shooting down their mothers and fathers in the streets (and not infrequently the children too), almost worked. What wrecked it was not any surfeit of compassion or regret for the acts of aggression the United States has committed there but the dawning realization that the mission of feeding the loathsome place could not be accomplished in the absence of inventing a government for it and inventing a government for it could not be done unless we also engaged in a protracted war with its natural rulers. By the end of last summer, the folly of Mr. Bush's legacy to his successor and the nation in thrusting the country into a minor war in Somalia was evident even to Republicans, and neither President Clinton nor her husband showed any desire to scuttle their unsteady vessel of state with further involvement there.

Nevertheless, despite such contretemps, the passion for global meddling continues. At the end of 1992, an article in *Foreign Policy* entitled "Saving Failed States" (a phrase used later by U.N. Ambassador Madeleine Albright to argue for continuing and escalated involvement in Somalia) postulated the compelling need for the United Nations and its largest province, the United States, to mount regular administrative and military escapades to salvage unsalvageable countries. Not only Somalia itself as well as the several non-countries of the Balkans but also Liberia and Cambodia were among the targets the authors identified for future missions of mercy, in addition to Ethiopia, Georgia (Stalin's, not Scarlett O'Hara's), and Zaire, with several other new nations of the old Soviet Union pitched in for good measure. In February of last year, the *New York Times* listed no fewer than 43 different countries into whose internal affairs the U.S./U.N. colossus ought to inject itself, and when Secretary of State Warren Christopher explained in his confirmation hearings before a patient Senate Foreign Relations Committee his philosophy of global do-good, he worried that unless the United States "did something," the world might soon witness the unprecedented horror of having "5,000 countries rather than the hundred plus we now have."

Why the prospect of 5,000 independent countries should be disturbing (I can think of at least 48 provinces of Washington that ought to be independent) Mr. Christopher did not explain, but the United Nations has been doing its best to make sure it doesn't happen. The number of U.N. troops involved in "peacekeeping" missions quadrupled in a single year between 1991 and the middle of 1992 from 11,000 to more than 44,000, as did the cost of fielding them, from the pittance of $700 million in 1991 to a whopping $2.8 billion in 1992, a quarter of which is disgorged by Americans.

Global reconstruction of states and countries that cannot function independently and probably should be swallowed by their neighbors is only one morsel on the globalist plate, however. The project of reconstruction — through military repression followed by the arrival of less lethal but no less destructive armies of educators, doctors, engineers, economists, goat and poultry experts, dam-builders, well-diggers, womanologists, childologists, vaccine scratchers, and ethnic relations managers — offers a bottomless pit of employment and empowerment for the therapeutic branch of the transnational elite, as well as rationales for more booty from the subordinate governments and peoples that pay for them. The creation of what Mr. Christopher called "a world where borders matter less and less, a world that demands we join with other nations to face challenges that range from overpopulation to AIDS to the very destruction of our planet's life support system" would also offer a bonanza for multinational corporations and the eat-and-swill-and-screw economy they promote. Last year also, *Time* magazine published a special Fall issue, largely financed by the Chrysler Corporation, burbling in glee over the arrival of a mono-cultural, mono-racial planet, and Pico Iyer in an essay called "The Global Village Finally Arrives," bubbled over the erasure of traditional cultures and countries by the planetary swarm of immigrants bound together through the chewing gum and chicken wire of global consumptionism. "In ways that were hardly conceivable even a generation ago," he wrote,

> the new world order is a version of the New World writ large ... A common multiculturalism links us all — call it Planet Hollywood, Planet Reebok or the United Colors of Benetton. ... The global village is defined, as we know, by an international youth culture that takes its cues from American pop culture. Kids in Perth and Prague and New Delhi are all tuning in to *Santa Barbara* on TV, and wriggling into 501 jeans, while singing to Madonna's latest in English. ... As fast as the world comes to America, America goes to the world — but it is an America that is itself multi-tongued and many hued.

Time's special issue appeared just on the eve of the passage of the North American Free Trade Agreement, a somewhat weaker U.S. analogue to the Maastricht treaty's continental unification of Europe, and the year closed with former Secretary of State James Baker, Jeane Kirkpatrick, and several other globocrats calling for the extension of NATO to encompass all of Europe, regardless of the minor detail that the disappearance of the Soviet Union and the Warsaw Pact, the *raisons d'être* of the Atlantic alliance, rendered NATO superfluous. Their arguments for expanding the Atlantic treaty, like the economic argument for NAFTA, were only pedantic sidebars to their real purpose, to nail down the planks of the New World Order in such a way that the principals could not escape from the transnational house they were constructing around themselves.

The temptation, to which writers on both the undomesticated right and left have readily succumbed, is to call the trend toward a global regime a form of imperialism, and apologists for the new planetary order like Charles Krauthammer afford some reason for doing so. Mr. Krauthammer has expressed no small skepticism about a Balkan engagement and no small disenchantment with the Somalian adventure, but only a few years ago in *The National Interest*, he was slobbering over the prospect of nothing less than "Universal Dominion" for the "West," an expression that to him seems to mean not much more than a global fast-food chain occasionally backed up by the Marines, and when he plumped for the United States "to wish and work for a super-sovereign West economically, culturally, and politically hegemonic in the world," it might not have been unreasonable to infer that he was advocating imperialism.

But in fact globalism is not at all the same thing as imperialism. In imperialism, at least the historic versions of it we know, a particular political and cultural unit expands and imposes itself and its power on other particular political and cultural units, as when Rome, Great Britain, or the United States conquered and controlled other countries and other territories. Up to a point, imperialism is a perfectly normal and natural (though not necessarily harmless) result of any successful state. If a state keeps winning its wars, if its subjects or citizens are economically successful, then sooner or later the state and its people will wind up with an empire, and typically the state then sends out some of those people to govern the empire, exploit it, and bring back lots of swag and ego-gratification for those remaining at home.

Globalism is rather different. Under globalism, the political and cultural unit that is expanding is not the city-state, nation, or people that expands under imperialism; indeed, the dynamic of globalism works to submerge and even destroy such particularities. What expands under globalism is the elite itself, which progressively disengages itself from the political and cultural unit from which it originated and becomes an autonomous force, a unit not subordinated or loyal to any particular state, people, or culture. In the globalist regime that is writhing toward birth today, the transnational elite that runs it does not even claim to be advancing the material or spiritual interests of the nations it uses; the elite has only contempt for national identity, regards national sovereignty as at best obsolete and at worst a barrier to its aspirations, and believes (or affects to believe) that nationality and all its characteristics are on the way out.

Economies, in the globalist mind, are already "global," so nations no longer possess distinct and conflicting economic interests. Populations also will and ought to be global, so nations no longer serve as the depositories of distinctive cultural identities carried by specific peoples and coupled to political expression, and there is only Mr. Iyer's planetary consumption culture of Reeboks and Madonna. Political interests too are supposedly joined together, so that we can now forget about territorial disputes between countries, centuries-old national hatreds, and geopolitical conflicts determined by the evolution of earth and sea. Today, in the globalist goo-goo land, the only interests that exist are common ones, such as curing AIDS and saving whales, which separate and sovereign nations can't pursue successfully by themselves.

But, while the transnational elite is busy persuading us that we have no collective interests as separate and distinct peoples, it neglects to point out the common interest that binds its own members and the organizational structures that house them — in multinational bureaucracies like those of the United Nations, the IMF, GATT, UNESCO, etc.; in multinational corporations; and in communications and educational institutions that are now transnational in reach and operations. Most of the "problems" the elite frets over, from curing AIDS and saving whales to pacifying Somalis and explaining to Serbs and Sinhalese the ethics of Bertrand Russell and Phil Donahue, are contrived to suit its own interests in gouging nations and their peoples for more money, conscripting their citizens into global legions to protect the elite and its projects, and locking itself into permanent power by diminishing the sovereignty and independence of nations and taking over the functions of their governments.

Lacking a morally convincing argument with which to clothe this naked grasp for power, the elite and its apologists make their case by appealing to drippy moral opacities and patching up such appeals with dubious claims of historical inevitability and irreversibility. But even a casual consideration of their claims exposes their weakness. Not long after the end of the Gulf War, Brian Urquhart, former U.N. undersecretary general and one of the Global Village's foremost town criers, announced in the *New York Times* that "The unraveling of national sovereignty seems to be a fixture of the post-Cold War era." The march to global rule is irreversible, you see, and we might as well get on with building upon it instead of trying to thwart it by shoring up the crumbling and illusory dikes of national sovereignty.

But of course what had unraveled was not sovereignty. What had unraveled was the denial of national sovereignty by the Soviet Empire, and what had proliferated and is proliferating today and will keep on proliferating is precisely the national sovereignty the transnational elite so despises and fears.

The main conflict in the world today is the struggle between the forces of nationalism — which encompasses and includes cultural, racial, tribal, religious, and other group loyalties and collectivities — and those of globalism, which includes the interests and ideologies of the elites who push globalism for their own benefit. It is a conflict that supersedes (but also to some degree encompasses) the truly obsolescent division between right and left. It is one that will not go away, no matter how many of Madonna's songs you listen to, and with the conjunction of nationalism and populism in the opposition to NAFTA, it is a conflict that is now beginning to erupt in the United States. If the United States has a future as anything more than the tax base and recruiting grounds for the transnational elite and its regime, the conflict between a popular nationalism and elite globalism will need to develop even more, as it will in other nations. What America needs today is its own General Mohammed Aideed, a leader willing and able to rally Americans in resistance to our own local branch of the elite, and what the rest of the planet needs is not more Bushes, Clintons, Christophers, Urquharts, Iyers, and Boutros Boutroses, but to let 5,000 national sovereignties bloom.

[March, 1994]

Religious Wrong

Despite the ocean of ink that has been spilled in the last several months on the "religious right," perhaps the most sensible comment that has thus far been uttered about it, or at least about its journalistic coverage and political analysis, was penned by John F. Persinos in an article published in the magazine *Campaigns and Elections* last September. "When examined with a coldly non-partisan eye," wrote Mr. Persinos, "it turns out that much of the mainstream's reportage on the Christian Right is a hodge-podge of cliches, regurgitated conventional wisdom, and fatuous analysis." Of course, there is hardly any subject that mainstream political journalism in this country touches of which the exact same thing could not be said, but there seems to be something about the combination of "religious" and "right" that encourages the construction of veritable monuments of the very kind of "fatuous analysis" of which Mr. Persinos was writing. There are, in my mind, two main reasons why American journalists and analysts so smashingly succeed in making fools of themselves whenever they talk about the "religious right."

In the first place, with the Clinton administration still in office, the political left needs an enemy against which it can rail for the purposes of raising money for its various causes, increasing the subscription levels of its magazines, and rallying the dozing voters to the tattered banners of liberal congressional candidates. The prospect of Falwell, Robertson, Buchanan, North, and Helms snooping into your bedroom, burning books in your local library, and outlawing lingerie advertisements in your local newspapers is probably enough to elicit a few dollars from even the most skin-flinted progressives, and, just as people on the political right have often resorted to similar tactics of scare and smear against their friends on the left, some liberal activists probably really believe their own propaganda about the religious right, a belief that contributes to the very kind of fatuity Mr. Persinos mentioned.

The other reason for the flood of rhetorical cow drop about the religious right is that, for a certain sort of mentality common on the left, the prospect of being persecuted is just too delicious to pass up. Leftism of all kinds often takes its moral energy from its own paranoia, its deeply rooted obsession that it stands alone against the forces of reaction and that those forces are on the eve of triumph, and while the left is invariably the first to head for the beaches when a real triumph of reaction actually takes place, to stand athwart the petty and usually harmless despots who try to close down local porno stores and to feel the nearly erotic stimulus that one is about to go to the stake oneself is always a lot of fun as well as immensely invigorating to the leftist ego.

We do not, therefore, need to look very far to find reasons for the yelling and screaming about the sinister emergence of the religious right to which the nation was obliged to listen last summer. Part of the hysteria was deliberately engineered simply for political and fund-raising purposes, and the engineering was successful precisely because most adherents of the left are both credulous enough to believe that an inquisitorial tide is about to engulf the country and self-important enough to imagine that they will be the first victims of the reaction. It is not remarkable, then, that the emergence of a religious right excites people on the secular left; what is remarkable, however, is that the religious right exists at all.

It is remarkable because not only is the United States today, like most economically developed societies everywhere, a largely secular culture but also because the American right itself has not until fairly recently expressed much interest in religion. Prior to World War II, hardly any major figure on the American right was significantly religious at all, and some were more or less outspoken enemies of religion in general and Christianity in particular. H.L. Mencken, Albert Jay Nock, and most of the group that Justin Raimondo identifies as the "Old Right" of the anti-New Deal, anti-interventionist orientation were not in the least concerned with religion except to mock it. Robert A. Taft, who generally reflected the political views of this movement as he led its political efforts, himself seems to have lived and died as a thoroughly conventional Episcopalian, a calling almost indistinguishable from outright heathenism. The considerably less libertarian persuasion grouped around the racialist right, including Lothrop Stoddard and Madison Grant, was explicitly anti-Christian, while the "American fascist" Lawrence Dennis (as well as Ezra Pound) were also either uninterested in religion or hostile to it. Even in the 1950s, the founder of the John Birch Society, Robert Welch, was a professing atheist whose personal hero was the Transcendentalist shaman Ralph Waldo Emerson, while Welch's one-time colleague, the late and brilliant Revilo P. Oliver, was as well-known for his bitterness toward what he called "Jesus juice" as he was for his animosity to Jews and their supposed conspiracy.

It was only in the post-World War II right, the right of William F. Buckley Jr. and the late Russell Kirk, that religion came to be closely linked with American conservatism. Part of this development was due to the general revival of religion in the post-War era that gave us such mainstream icons of holiness as Billy Graham and Norman Vincent Peale and the cult of "civic religion" in the 50s, but part of it also was due to the emergence of anti-communism as a central issue of the right, as well as a dawning perception that what was occurring in the West as well as under communism was not simply a violation of the fundamental institutional cátegories of the civilization of the West but an implicit abandonment of and an ever-more explicit attack on them. It is hardly surprising, given the victimization of Christianity and Christians by the communists, that Christian clergymen and thinkers were in the forefront of anti-communist movements, that they imparted their theological commitments to their political and social commentary, and that their thought mainly identified the West and its survival with Christianity rather than with other staples of conservative concern such as property and the free market, constitutionalism and the rule of law, nationality, race, or social hierarchy.

But conservative intellectualism, whatever thoughts it entertained about religion, had little practical or political impact either before or after World War II, and the emergence of the religious right in the 70s owes little to the abstruse theology, obscure liturgical controversies, and head-spinning political theory with which so many conservative eggheads occupied themselves in the 50s and '60s. What its emergence does have to do with is a socio-political phenomenon that is far broader and far more significant as a world-historical force than either organized conservatism or the religious right itself perceives.

The "religious right" is merely the current incarnation of the on-going Middle American Revolution, a cultural and political movement that has underlain the political efforts of the American right since the end of World War II. Despite what many right-wing sages would like to believe, that movement never had much to do with their perennial holy cow, the free market, but rather with the perception that the white middle-class core of American society and culture was being evicted from its historic position of cultural and political dominance and was in fact in process of becoming an exploited and repressed proletariat. It was this perception, rudimentary as it was, that to a large extent underlay the political movements around Father Coughlin, Huey Long, and similar figures in the Depression and later around Sen. McCarthy, whose anti-communist radicalism is explicable only as a vehicle for Middle American resistance to and resentment of the ruling class that had by the 1950s displaced the traditional bourgeois elite of the nation.

Since the end of World War II, the American right as a mass political force in the United States has been driven by three successive causes. The first, anti-communism, carried not only McCarthy but also Dwight Eisenhower and Richard Nixon in the 1950s, though Eisenhower merely piggy-backed on the synthesis of anti-communism and Middle American class and ethnic consciousness that Nixon and McCarthy had so brilliantly forged. The second, opposition to the civil rights revolution based mainly in the South and later in northern white working-class suburbs, carried Barry Goldwater, George Wallace and (again) Richard Nixon, though Mr. Goldwater never understood what he was leading and continues to this day to imagine that it was a movement for "individual freedom" (a delusion that helped him lose the support of northern working-class voters) rather than a social convulsion for the preservation of class, ethnic, and cultural dominance.

The third cause of the right is now and has been what was called in the 1970s the "social issue" and in the '90s the "cultural war," and, far more explicitly and effectively than the earlier anti-communism and bourgeois individualism espoused by the right of the '50s and '60s, it focuses on resisting the erosion of traditional morality and the traditional middle-class social and economic dominance the morality codified. "Cultural" issues were indeed present in but remained largely tangential to the right-wing efforts of the earlier decades and emerged as prevalent concerns only in reaction to the cultural assaults of the 60s and afterwards. The most obvious way to defend a moral code is through religion, and the most obvious people to defend it are religious leaders and their followers. Hence, religion emerged logically as the appropriate vehicle for the expression of Middle American moral, social, and cultural counter-revolution.

What follows from this line of analysis of the religious right as it exists today is that what ultimately drives its adherents is not religion in the ordinary sense. What drives them is the perception — accurate in my view — that the culture their religion reflects and defends is withering and that that withering portends a disaster for themselves, their class, their country and their civilization. Religion happens to be a convenient vehicle for their otherwise unarticulated and perfectly well-founded fears. But while it is a convenient vehicle and a more effective one than those that carried the right in earlier days, it is not the most effective vehicle the right could have.

This is not to say that the religious right is composed of hypocrites who use religion for political ends. With the possible exception of most of its more prominent leaders, it's not. Most adherents of the religious right are sincerely and seriously religious; but you can be sincerely and seriously religious without being political and without being political in the way the religious right is. It's not religion that drives; it's the legitimate frustrations of a social class that has been bludgeoned and betrayed by its established leaders for more than 50 years.

Religion is not the most effective political and ideological vehicle for expressing and publicly vindicating the frustrations that animate the Middle American Revolution because the Christianity of the right simply doesn't encompass very many Middle American interests. While the religious right is effectively armed with an ideology and a world-view that enhances its militancy, its energy in mounting effective political and cultural opposition at the local level, and its alienation from the dominant elite and the elite's regime in the leviathan state, the movement's aims remain too limited.

The real problem with the religious right is that, in the long run, its religious vehicle won't carry it home. If they ever ended abortion, restored school prayer, outlawed sodomy and banned pornography, I suspect, most of its followers would simply declare victory and retire. But having accomplished all of that, the Christian right would have done absolutely nothing to strip the federal government of the power it has seized throughout this century, restore a proper understanding and enforcement of the Constitution and of republican government, prevent the inundation of the country by anti-Western immigrants, stop the cultural and racial dispossession of the historic American people, or resist the absorption of the American nation into a multicultural and multiracial globalist regime. Indeed, the Christian Right for the most part doesn't care about these issues or even perceive them as issues, and in so far as it does, it not infrequently lines up on the wrong side of them.

Yet these are the principal lines of conflict in the Middle American Revolution, and it is by winning on them, rather than on school prayer and creationism, that Middle American interests will be served and the incumbent ruling class and its power apparatus overthrown. While the purely religious perspective of the Christian Right helps to radicalize it more than anti-communism, libertarianism, or other and older ideologies of the right did, it also tends to narrow the vision of what really demands a radical challenge from the right — the domination of a hostile ruling class that uses state power to entrench itself and wreck the country, the culture and the middle class as well. Thus, the religious orientation of the Christian Right serves to create what Marxists like to call a "false consciousness" for Middle Americans, an ideology that appeals to and mobilizes a socio-political class but which does not accurately codify the objective interests and needs of the class and in the end only distracts and deflects its political action and ultimately works to buttress and reinforce the dominant regime.

What is needed now is not a vehicle that will trap the right into a large but limited cultural and political ghetto but one that can steer it toward an authentic and serious understanding of the real needs of the Middle Americans who are attracted to the Christian Right as well as others who are repelled by it but increasingly perceive how they are exploited and misruled by the elite. If a movement should appear that could articulate that kind of vision, then, religious or not in its focus, it could successfully mobilize and lead the core of the nation and the civilization as it needs and ought to be led.

[December, 1994]

Racialpolitik

Whatever it is that the emerged Republican majority does with the immense congressional power it seized in last November's elections, it will probably be unimportant compared to the force that has just started emerging in the same elections and which the national leadership of the Republican Party, and even more the Democratic Party, sedulously tried to ignore, deny, denounce, and destroy. The emergence of the Republican majority, of course, is important in terms of the conventional politics of the nation. Not only has it converted the remaining tenure of the Clinton administration into a two-year-long sequel to *Night of the Living Dead*, this time with the zombies lurching around murderously in the Oval Office, but also it represents the effective end of the New Deal electoral coalition and a great leap forward in the political consciousness of the Middle American Revolution.

By themselves those two developments are enough to make the elections of 1994 a major event in American history. But the end of the coalition that formed the electoral foundation of 20th century liberalism does not necessarily mean that a genuinely anti-liberal coalition has permanently crystallized, nor does the Republican victory mean the Republicans are authentic or adequate leaders of the revolution from which they have gained at least temporary congressional dominance.

Since its inception in the 19th century, the Republican Party has been wedded to the myth of Economic Man, the myth that holds that the desire for material gain is the principal if not the only muscle that throbs in the human breast and that therefore all historical events can be adequately explained in terms of economic motivation. Most Republicans are probably not aware that they share this myth with unemployed Russian Marxists and too-long-employed American college professors, but the persistence of the myth in what passes for the Republican mind is evident in last year's "Contract with America," with all its budget-balancing, tax-cutting, welfare-reforming, economic incentive proposals. It remains to be seen how many of the "Contract's" actual promises the Republican leadership was serious about, how much the leadership and the party will be able or willing to enact, and how much is even possible to implement, given what seem to be some of its glaring contradictions. But even if all of the Contract sails through Congress, escapes the ignominious fate of a veto from the nation's First Zombie, and latches itself onto the American way of life as firmly as sit-coms and Social Security, it will do little to fill the tank of what is now rapidly becoming the principal motor of the Middle American Revolution.

That motor, the force that the established leadership of both parties sought to smother, is, in a word, race, and it is evident in the controversy over the most controversial issue in the November elections, California's Proposition 187. That proposition was far more controversial than Ollie North or the role of the religious right, and unlike them, it will remain with us, shaping the practical politics and the impractical political conversation of the nation, for decades to come.

Ostensibly, of course, 187 was not at all about race but merely a proposal to prohibit illegal aliens from obtaining public services, mainly welfare, public education, and non-emergency public health care, but as is often the case with political issues, what the ballot measure ostensibly was about is not what it really was about. The racial meaning of the measure became clear as the day for the vote approached, with mass rallies of thousands of Hispanics waving Mexican flags, occupying public buildings, screaming at policemen and anyone else who attracted their attention, and vocally threatening to burn the cities and the state to cinders if Americans dared vote contrary to the passions of the mobs. On at least one occasion, they beat up an elderly American who had the courage to sport the American flag in expressing his support of 187. The man was luckier than the flag he bore, which the mob promptly burned. These were clear expressions of a militant non-white and anti-American racial consciousness, which the press invariably described as "peaceful." Just to show how peaceful they were, the National Guard and the Los Angeles Police Department were placed on full alert in the event that Prop 187 actually passed.

In the event, of course, 187 passed overwhelmingly by 59 percent to 41 percent, but it is in the ethnic and racial breakdown of the vote that the meaning of the proposition for the emergence of racial consciousness is most evident. From exit polls conducted by the *Los Angeles Times* during the voting, it appears that 63 percent of white Californians supported 187, while 53 percent of blacks, 53 percent of Asians, and a whopping 77 percent of Hispanics opposed it. The racial division is obvious: Non-whites voted together in opposing a measure that was portrayed, almost entirely by its foes, as racially driven, while whites, who still make up 81 percent of the California electorate, supported it by what is usually regarded as a landslide margin. The racial division is evident also in the breakdown of the national vote, in which 63 percent of white men supported the Republicans. As Thomas Edsall wrote in the *Washington Post* shortly after the election, the mass defection of white males to the GOP "violates a core concept at the heart of the Democratic Party as the party of working people. White men are those experiencing the largest wage declines, the brunt of defense cutbacks and the dramatic attenuation of corporate loyalty."

The racial meaning of the vote for 187 is hardly surprising with respect to non-whites. For years now, politically organized non-white minorities in the United States have openly boasted of their racial consciousness, developed nationally powerful lobby groups to represent their interests, and have effectively legitimized the belief that it is their right to think, feel, vote, and behave as members of their own racial identity while delegitimizing the same belief for whites. Many, indeed perhaps most, whites have permitted this development and even encouraged or supported it, though some more aggressively than others. But what the vote for 187 tells us about whites is that they are now starting to vote for their own interests as a racial group, in opposition to the interests of other races. If that trend continues, and there is every reason to believe it will, what it logically implies is the emergence of an overtly racial politics in the United States of the kind that we have not seen before.

Of course, not all whites supported 187, and most prominent among those who actually attacked it were presidential perennial Jack Kemp and Bill "Mr. Virtue" Bennett himself. The two neo-conservatives hastened to California to harangue the masses with their insight that "the American national identity is not based on ethnicity, or race, or national origin, or religion. The American national identity is based on a creed, on a set of principles and ideas." Of course, that is a common view of the American identity, one that has been repeatedly expressed throughout our history, though there are at least two problems with it. In the first place it happens to be untrue. In the second place it happens to be a dangerous and even suicidal claim.

It is untrue because the major fact about American national identity is that it is an identity created by British settlers and later European immigrants and therefore is almost exclusively the achievement of whites. Whatever wise pleasantries of universalism may turn up in the patriotic oratory and public documents of American history, no one can claim that the American identity is really the kind of watery abstraction the Kemp-Bennett statement purports it to be. Behind and beneath those pleasantries lie the concrete identity, experience, and aspirations of a homogeneous people "of a common blood," as Jefferson put it in his draft of the Declaration of Independence, and to reduce that essentially racial as well as cultural heritage to the bloodless "principles and ideals" that Mr. Kemp and Mr. Bennett busy themselves tooting is not only a confession of the most dismal ignorance but also a trumpeting of the most brazen betrayal.

Moreover, the Kemp-Bennett claim is dangerous because it fundamentally misunderstands the nature of a nation or of any collective political identity other than a debating society. If indeed being an American were "based on a creed, on a set of principles and ideas," then any person in the world who adhered to that creed would be an American. That might be fine with the open borders crowd whom the Kemp-Bennett statement was designed to please, but it also means that any person who does not adhere to the creed is not an American, and in asserting the credal identity of the United States, the Kemp-Bennett statement comes close to formulating the grounds of a new totalitarianism. The Soviet Union was "based on a creed," and Russians who dissented from the creed were punished severely. How else indeed could a state defining itself through a creed cohere? So far from opening the national gates to anyone who wants to come here, defining American national identity in terms of a creed actually guarantees a closed and perhaps brutally repressive regime and implies nothing whatsoever about what kind of welcome we might give to immigrants.

In the first place, if you believe in the Creed, you can be a perfectly good American in the slums of Buenos Aires or the jungles of Rwanda, just as you can be a perfectly good Christian or a perfectly good libertarian or a perfectly good communist, and there's no reason at all for you to come here or go anywhere. In the second place, if adhering to the Creed is what makes you an American, then why not give creed tests to all immigrants, or indeed to native Americans, and if they don't subscribe to the Gospel according to Jack and Bill, round 'em up and send 'em back. No one knows what any of the immigrants to this country, legal or illegal, past or present, believe or have believed, and there is no reason for anyone to be examined or tested as to what they believe before being admitted. The credal basis of national identity that Mr. Kemp and Mr. Bennett blather about may sound both high-minded and broad-minded, but upon any but the most superficial examination, it (like so much else of what they have to say) turns out to be transparently false and, if it were taken any more seriously than most of the slogans and bumper-stickers that pass for high political theory among neo-conservatives, could serve as the basis of a far more restrictive regime than any nativist has ever conceived.

Despite the defection of white neo-conservatives and the left, the emergence of an overtly racial politics among whites in the vote for 187 suggests that in the future, race will become a significant element in what it means to be an American at all, and that is hardly unprecedented. As the late M.E. Bradford pointed out in an essay on immigration, the very first congressional naturalization statute in 1790 restricted American citizenship to "any alien, being a free white person," and Bradford commented that "all of the Framers clearly expected that it would be Europeans who presented themselves for 'membership' here." Stephen Douglas, in his opening shot in the Lincoln-Douglas debates, could say to the cheers of his Illinois audience that "I believe this government was made on the white basis. I believe it was made by white men for the benefit of white men and their posterity forever, and I am in favor of confining the citizenship to white men — men of European birth and European descent, instead of conferring it upon Negroes and Indians, and other inferior races." Douglas, of course, won the election, though his opponent did all he could to persuade the voters that he didn't disagree on such points. As late as 1965, the federal immigration code restricted immigration on the basis of "national origin" (largely a circumlocution for race), and as Lawrence Auster has shown, the repeal of the law was possible only because supporters of repeal denied it would alter the ethnic and racial composition of the nation.

The vote for Proposition 187 goes far to relegitimize the racial aspect of the American national identity, and the overwhelming white support for the measure suggests that an overt racial identity is now emerging as part of Middle American political and cultural consciousness. If other races and ethnic groups can identify themselves and act in terms of their own racial identities, it should hardly surprise them and their white allies that whites themselves sooner or later will also begin to do so. But the larger meaning of the emergence of racial politics in America is that it directly challenges the myth of Economic Man in which both the left and the right cloak themselves. Their own allegiance to that myth is the real reason why Mr. Kemp and Mr. Bennett denounced 187 so bitterly and why the Republican Party as a whole finds immigration such a difficult issue. The emergence of racialpolitik means that there is something besides material gain that drives human beings, and those who adhere to the mythology of Economic Man have no room for that something in their world-view. As racial consciousness begins to mature among white Americans as it has among non-whites, therefore, Economic Man and those elites that work for him are likely to find themselves in the ranks of the permanently unemployed.

[February, 1995]

Voices in the Air

By the middle of the second month of the Republican Revolution, acute obervers were beginning to see that the revolution might actually go somewhere if only the Republicans weren't in charge of it. Aside from such irritating contretemps as the discussions of Speaker Newt Gingrich's book deal, his instantaneous dumping of historian Christina Jeffries when her criticisms of a curriculum on the Nazi persecution of European Jews came to light, and his irrepressible habit of unbosoming his every thought and neurological reflex to a bewildered press and citizenry, the prospects of the revolution dimmed considerably when Mr. Gingrich and his counterpart in the Senate, Bob Dole, eagerly signed on to the bailout of a bankrupt Mexico and began to back away from some of their own revolution's commitments.

Mr. Gingrich had second thoughts about ending welfare for immigrants, despite the obvious popular support for doing so, and second thoughts again about repealing the notorious "assault weapons" ban enacted with Republican help in the last months of the previous Congress, despite the obvious debt of the new Republican majority to the votes of outraged gunowners. On all these issues — the bailout, the immigrants, and guns — he was obliged by pressures from within his own party, especially freshmen Republicans considerably to the right of him and Mr. Dole, to reverse himself yet again and exude third thoughts. But since exuding thoughts is never difficult for the

Speaker, his political ping-pong was not the main problem.

On the more substantive commitments of the party to its "Contract with America" there was definite progress, though many rank and file Republicans and conservatives asked themselves exactly why the Contract's sometimes arcane pledges were important at all. Several items in the Contract involving rather radical constitutional changes threatened to turn what remains of the U.S. Constitution into the kind of voluminous and indecipherable document more familiar to such governments as those of Bolivia and Botswana, and even with a Republican majority in the House, some parts of the Contract could not pass without suffering amputation of their more radical and meaningful provisions. Nor was there any language in the Contract that committed its signatories to the wholesome task of eliminating whole departments and agencies of the federal leviathan, abolishing affirmative action, or reversing the ruin inflicted on the Republic by generations of judicial insanity, though individual Republican members or Senators did mutter about engaging these issues on their own.

Revolutions, however, exhaust themselves rather quickly, even when fed by passions and ideological fixations considerably fiercer than those known to drive the souls of Republicans, and by locking the House and Senate on the immediate goal of enacting the Contract's promises, the Republican leadership may have ensured that any further and more substantial radical proclivities in Republican breasts would be smothered before they had a chance to squeak. Indeed, even as the 104th Congress convened to begin implementing the revolution, it was advised by its self-appointed egghead, Bill Kristol, to eschew serious reforms from the right until the Republicans had also captured the presidency. The Republicans, it seems, were about as ready for their own revolution as a college freshman is to start studying for his final exams.

Yet the main problem with the Republican Revolution comes not from the questionable conduct or judgment of its leaders or from any lack of legislative skills. The main problem is simply that the Republican Party finds it almost impossible to conceive of public policies and legislation in anything but economic terms, that it remains wedded to the world-view associated with the myth of Economic Man. No matter how often Republicans dip their knees to "family values," the religious right, and "cultural issues," and no matter how much they exploit patriotic sentiment by contriving to nominate such military titans as Ulysses S. Grant or Colin Powell for president, it is only when dollars and cents are being talked about that the Republican eye begins to gleam and the Republican lip trembles with lachrymose enthusiasm.

The myth of Economic Man, like myths in general, is today less a consciously embraced theory of human nature and history than an intellectual archaism from the bourgeois order of the 19th century, when the Republicans led the nation in crushing a region that did not embrace the myth and proceeded to construct what was essentially the "Second Republic" of American history between the Civil War and the New Deal. Perhaps the only wise sentence that John Maynard Keynes ever uttered was his well-known insight, at the end of his *General Theory of Employment, Interest, and Money*, that "Practical men, who believe themselves to be quite exempt from any intellectual influences, are usually the slaves of some defunct economist. Madmen in authority, who hear voices in the air, are distilling their frenzy from some academic scribbler of a few years back. I am sure that the power of vested interests is vastly exaggerated compared with the gradual encroachment of ideas." Leaving aside his skepticism about the power of vested interests (a skepticism rather implausible when the Mexican bailout is considered), Lord Keynes could have been describing (and may have been describing) the Republican Party of the 20th century.

The myth of Economic Man, in so far as it can be accurately expressed, holds that human beings are driven mainly or even exclusively by considerations of material gain and loss, and therefore that the key to understanding history is the calculation of which economic interests prevail and what those interests are. From that dubious generalization, its adherents elicit a moral imperative, that economic calculations should prevail, and that therefore the value of any course of action, especially public policies, should be judged in terms of whether and how much they enhance material gain. This myth and its derivatives are the foundation stones of both socialism (especially its Marxist version) and capitalism, and it is no accident that Karl Marx was as indebted to the classical economists who helped unleash the myth on the modern mind as he was enchanted by the American Civil War and the Second Republic it initiated as progressive forward steps of world-historical significance. The main practical difference between the socialist and capitalist versions of the myth is simply that each perceives different roads toward their shared goals of the full dinner pail. It tells us something about both communists and Republicans that they think utopia consists of eating out of a bucket.

In the case of Republicans, almost all of the principal contents of the Contract with America have to do with explicitly economic issues — the balanced budget amendment, the line item veto, unfunded mandates, welfare reform, tax reform, and even the proposal to alter the accounting method by which U.S. participation in U.N. peacekeeping missions is calculated. Popular discontent with immigration is conveniently dismissed as mere racial scapegoating provoked by economic dislocations, and immigration itself is seen as entirely the result of economic dysfunctions in Mexico and Latin America. Change the economy, and both immigration and opposition to it will go away. The whole debate over immigration is conventionally conducted only in terms of whether it is good or bad for the American economy, not whether it will alter the basic shape of the national culture. The conventional explanations of urban crime and welfare dependency also are that they are the results of economic incentives foolishly created by urban policies that ignore the universal economic motors of human nature. Create the right incentives through enterprise zones and Project HOPE and we'll end crime, welfare, and poverty. The debates over NAFTA and GATT also were largely confined to their effects on the economy rather than their impact on national sovereignty, and indeed the myth of Economic Man implies that nations themselves are insignificant compared to the appetites for accumulation that drive human individuals.

Hence, it is not surprising that the prophecies of Karl Marx and Friedrich Engels in *The Communist Manifesto* about the disappearance of the nation-state closely resemble what Mr. Gingrich's main guru, Alvin Toffler, predicts in his pop futurist best-seller, *The Third Wave*. "The workingmen have no country," preached the fathers of communism. "National differences and antagonisms between peoples are daily more and more vanishing, owing to the development of the bourgeoisie, to freedom of commerce, to the world market, to uniformity in the mode of production and in the conditions of life corresponding thereto." Mr. Toffler essentially agrees, writing "it is questionable how effectively national borders can be sealed off — or for how long. For the shift toward a Third Wave industrial base requires the development of a highly ramified, sensitive, wide open 'neural network' or information system, and attempts by individual nations to dam up data flows may interfere with, rather than accelerate, their own economic development. All such developments — the new economic problems, the new environmental problems, and the new communications technologies — are converging to undermine the position of the nation-state in the global scheme of things."

Of course, in the global scheme of things, just the opposite has come true. Marx's workingmen enthusiastically supported the belligerent nationalisms of World War I, and the collapse of communism and the end of the Cold War have witnessed a nationalist renaissance on every continent. What is interesting about the false predictions, however, is that they were based on economic calculations, and the persistence of nationalist sentiments and energies simply didn't fit into the equations of either prophet.

Whether consciously or not, the friends of Economic Man simply ignore and omit from their calculations, analyses, projections, prophecies, and policies whatever doesn't fit the mythological assumptions from which their schemes evolve, and therefore they are always shocked to witness mass movements that ignore economic interests and center around charismatic leaders, traditional but practically useless symbols and images, and imperatives that demand exertions that make no economic sense, the postponement of immediate gratification, the denial of sensual satisfactions, and the sacrifice of life itself. Nor can public policies based on this mythology encompass very many of the social realities around which human existence revolves.

Obviously, economic interests and economic issues are important, and they are important grounds for evaluating the success of a society or its government; but the coronation of Economic Man as the absolute monarch of modern political thought not only ignores and distorts human reality but also serves to destroy and erase human social and cultural realities the monarch doesn't much care for anyway. Relying on "the market" as the universal answer to every question of public discussion, the adherents of Economic Man merely accelerate the institutional destruction out of which the power of the mass state emerges as an alternative answer to the questions Economic Men skip over. While Republicans worship at the temple of Economic Man, two prominent social critics from the left have recently noted the social destructiveness the cult promotes.

Thus, historian Eugene Genovese in a sympathetic critique of *The Southern Tradition* remarks that "southern conservatives understand the contradictions that neither Ronald Reagan nor George Bush nor even [!] William Buckley has faced squarely. Capitalism has historically been the greatest solvent of traditional social relations. Ronald Reagan has had every right to celebrate capitalism as the greatest revolutionary force in world history...." Similarly, the late Christopher Lasch writes in his posthumous *The Revolt of the Elites* that "The market notoriously tends to universalize itself. It does not easily coexist with institutions that operate according to principles antithetical to itself — schools and universities, newspapers and magazines, charities, families. Sooner or later the market tends to absorb them all. It puts an almost irresistible pressure on every activity to justify itself in the only terms it recognizes: to become a business proposition, to pay its own way, to show black ink on the bottom line. It turns news into entertainment, scholarship into professional careerism, social work into scientific management of poverty. Inexorably it remodels every institution in its own image."

Having enthroned policies informed by the mythologies of the market and Economic Man, Republicans are always amazed to discover that the results are not at all what they predicted and that those who contributed their support to what was advertised as a revolution wanted something other than business as usual. Not only does the myth in which Republican minds are swaddled not even acknowledge the non-economic forces that really drive the popular base of their revolution but also the myth serves to create new dislocations and destructions that the champions of the mass state will exploit to their own advantage. It should not therefore be surprising that the revolution the Republicans have promised us will stall before it leaves its garage and that it will turn out to be no revolution at all. Whoever the academic scribblers from whom the Republican Revolutionaries have distilled their frenzy might be, what they are really enthroning is not at all different from the forces to which we have been enslaved since the days of Karl Marx and the revolutionary destruction of the Old Republic he celebrated.

[May, 1995]

From Household to Nation:
The Middle American Populism of Pat Buchanan

If there were any major difference between the presidential campaign of Pat Buchanan in 1996 and his first run at the Republican nomination in 1992, it was the relative calm with which his enemies greeted the announcement of his second candidacy and his rapid rise last year to the forefront of the Republican field. Rabbi Avi Weiss and his goon platoons still found time and someone else's money to dog Buchanan's steps from New Hampshire to California, and occasionally some other hired thug, usually a failed neo-conservative politician, would emerge from the political graveyard to moan ominously about Buchanan's "fascism," his "nativism" or his "racism." But in general, even Buchanan's most left-wing critics found the man himself likeable and many of his ideas compelling. Tom Carson of the *Village Voice* traveled with the Buchanan Brigades in Iowa last spring, and despite the agony of enduring a couple of weeks slumming in the Heartland, he could not help but be drawn to the popular insurgency the candidate was mounting. "I've been waiting my whole life for someone running for president to talk about the Fortune 500 as the enemy," Mr. Carson says he told Buchanan, "and when I finally get my wish, it turns out to be you."

Of course, there was criticism. In the early stages, its main thrust — from conservatives — was that he could not possibly win the nomination, let alone the election, and that his image as a fringe candidate, the notorious organizational weaknesses persisting from the 1992 campaign, and the lack of adequate money this time would stop him from becoming any more than a divisive vote-taker from real winners like Phil Gramm. By the end of the year, of course, the Texas Republican had largely faded from the discussion, though his bottomless pit of contributions kept him in the race. The more recent polls show Buchanan leading or matching Gramm in key early contest states like New Hampshire and Iowa, and by last summer Pat's fund-raising was outstripping that of the Texan's opulent money machine. It was beginning to look as though the boys who put their dollar on Mr. Gramm had backed the wrong pony.

But despite Buchanan's emergence as a major candidate, few serious observers believed he could win the nomination, let alone the election, and that belief itself, widespread among conservatives preoccupied with getting rid of Bill Clinton, threatened to become a self-fulfilling prophecy. For those on the right who want only to oust the incumbent resident of the White House or impress their friends with invitations to the court soirees of the next Republican successor to the presidential purple, winning the election is all that matters, and Buchanan's supposed unelectability was enough to make them lose interest. But the courtiers and professional partisans miss the larger victory the Buchanan campaign is on the eve of winning. If Buchanan loses the nomination, it will be because his time has not yet come, but the social and political forces on which both his campaigns have been based will not disappear, and even if he does lose, he will have won a secure and significant place in history as an architect of the victory those forces will eventually build.

The importance of the Buchanan campaign consists not in its capacity to win the nomination or the national election but in its organization of those forces into a coherent political coalition. That coalition includes the remnants of the "Old Right," as well as various single issue constituencies (pro-lifers, anti-immigration activists, protectionists) to which Buchanan is one of the few nationally recognized voices to speak. But it would be a serious error to squeeze Buchanan into a rigorously orthodox conservative pigeonhole from which he is merely trying to lead a replay of the Goldwater campaign, the candidacies of John Ashbrook or Phil Crane, or the Reagan movement, and especially in the last year he has expressed and developed ideas with which most adherents of the conventional American Right — mainstream conservative, paleo-conservative, or libertarian — are not entirely comfortable.

But conventional conservative doctrines today are virtually extinct politically, for the simple reason that the social groups that found them expressive of their interests and values no longer exist or no longer are able to command a significant political following, and as a result, conservative ideological candidates like Alan Keyes or Robert Dornan who insist on campaigning on those doctrines rise no higher than 2-3 percent in the polls. One major reason for the underestimation of Buchanan's prospects and for the surprise with which most analysts have greeted his unexpected success lay in their mistaken assumption that Buchanan was simply yet another right-wing protestor, calling the party and those parts of the nation that would listen to him to pick up the torch of doctrine and wave it until the waters of political and cultural darkness extinguished it. The major reason Buchanan has not been submerged is that the torch he carries illuminates new social forces that only now are forming a common political consciousness. What is important about these forces is not that a campaign centered on them does not now win major elections (indeed, it would be a fatal error if they succeeded in winning prematurely) but that the Buchanan campaign for the first time in recent history offers them an organized mode of expression that will allow them to develop and mature their consciousness and their power.

Those forces consist, of course, of the broad social and cultural spectrum of Middle America, which is not necessarily identical to the middle class (today largely an income stratum rather than a cultural unit) and is mainly distinguished by its location on the receiving end of the fused political, economic, and cultural apparatus of the dominant elites in the United States. Middle American political consciousness is instigated by the elites' systematic exploitation of those Middle American groups that are, at first gradually and now more and more rapidly, coming to perceive their exploitation and the real source of it. The exploitation functions on several fronts — economically, by hypertaxation and the design of a globalized economy dependent on exports and services in place of manufacturing; culturally, by the managed destruction of Middle American norms and institutions; and politically, by the regimentation of Middle Americans under the federal leviathan that serves as the keystone of the whole system of domination by which elites within and without the national government preserve their power.

The significant polarization within American society and the significant political conflict to which the emergence of Middle American radicalism points is between the elites, increasingly unified as a ruling class that relies on the national state as its principal instrument of power, and Middle America itself, which lacks the technocratic and managerial skills that yield control of the machinery of power. Other polarities and conflicts within American society — between religious and secular, white and black, national and global, worker and management — are beginning to fit into this larger polarity of Middle American and Ruling Class. The Ruling Class uses and is used by secularist, globalist, and anti-white and anti-Western forces for its and their advantage. Middle Americans are increasingly aware of the distinctions that separate them from the Ruling Class, increasingly aware of the strategies of domination and exploitation by which the Ruling Class rules, increasingly aware of their own victimization by the Ruling Class and its allies, and (most importantly) increasingly aware of a common determination to resist and destroy the power of the Ruling Class.

The interests that drive Middle American social and political forces are considerably different from those that drove the groups that generally supported one or another versions of "conservatism" in the era during and after the New Deal. Old Right conservatism was a body of ideas that appealed mainly to *haute bourgeois* businessmen and their localized, middle class adherents, a social base that 20th century social and economic transformations effectively wiped out. Old Right conservatism defended a limited, decentralized, and largely neutral national government and the ethic of small-town, small-business, Anglo-Saxon Protestantism. As the social base of the Old Right withered in the post-Depression and post-World War II era, the political and intellectual right essentially divorced itself from these declining interests and forces and evolved new and far less socially rooted ideologies that represented almost no one outside the narrow academic and journalistic circles that formulated them.

By the 50s and '60s, "movement" conservatives habitually quibbled with each other over the subtler points of their doctrines like late medieval Scholastic theologians, and the doctrines themselves — a bastardized libertarianism that only vaguely resembled its more rooted classical liberal and Old Whig ancestors, globalist anti-communism that slowly garbed itself in the costumes of Wilsonian democratism, and increasingly abstruse metaphysical and theological ponderosities — attracted none but dissident intellectuals and proved useless as vehicles for transporting a mass political following to electoral victory. Neo-conservatism, emerging in the late 60s and early 70s, was even worse. Far less cerebral than the esoteric abstractions churned out by 50s conservative intellectualism but considerably quicker on the draw when it came to political showdowns, neo-conservatism gained the adherence of no one but still other disgruntled eggheads alienated from the establishment left and contemptuous of their new-found allies on the right.

Given the collapse of the social base of the right and the addiction of right-wing intellectuals to ideological navel-gazing, the political right ceased to be able to develop serious political strategies. All it could do was pick up odd clusters of voters who were fearful of crime, resentful of racial integration, worried about communist take-overs, eager to remove federal fingers from their pockets, or passionate about the defense of business interests, the last subject never straying far from what remained of the right-wing mind. One way or another, the right managed to keep congressional seats and occasionally win the odd presidential election, but its victories were flukish, depending on the foibles of the opposition, and it was unable either to penetrate or dislodge the dominant culture created by the left or to win the firm allegiance of Middle Americans. There was enough in the rhetoric of Richard Nixon's "New Majority" and Ronald Reagan's appeal to Southern and blue-collar Democrats to stitch together momentary triumphs, but the persistent residues of pro-business conservative ideology and the failure to deliver on social and cultural commitments to Middle American constituencies prevented the consolidation of an enduring coalition with real roots in existing social forces and the culture those forces supported.

Middle American forces, emerging from the ruins of the old independent middle and working classes, found conservative, libertarian, and pro-business Republican ideology and rhetoric irrelevant, distasteful, and even threatening to their own socio-economic interests. The post-World War II middle class was in reality an affluent proletariat, economically dependent on the federal government through labor codes, housing loans, educational programs, defense contracts, and health and unemployment benefits. All variations of conservative doctrine rejected these as illegitimate extensions of the state and not infrequently boasted of plans to abolish most of them, and Middle American allegiance to political parties and candidates espousing such doctrine could never become firm. Yet, at the same time, the Ruling Class proved unable to uproot the social, cultural, and national identities and loyalties of the Middle American proletariat, and Middle Americans found themselves increasingly alienated from the political left and its embrace of anti-national policies and counter-cultural manners and morals.

Thus, there emerged a chronic Middle American political dilemma: While the left could win Middle Americans through its economic measures, it lost them through its social and cultural radicalism, and while the right could attract Middle Americans through appeals to law and order and defense of sexual normality, conventional morals and religion, traditional social institutions, and invocations of nationalism and patriotism, it only lost Middle Americans whenever it began to rehearse its old bourgeois economic formulas. Middle American votes could be won by whichever side of the political spectrum was more effectively able to agitate Middle American anxieties over cultural rot or economic catastrophe, but neither an increasingly anti-national and counter-cultural left nor an increasingly pro-business right could expect to stabilize Middle American political loyalties sufficiently to sustain a successful national coalition.

The persistence of the division of the political spectrum into "right" and "left" has therefore served to prevent the formation of a distinct Middle American political consciousness and the emergence of a new identity that synthesizes both the economic interests and cultural-national loyalties of the post-bourgeois proletarianized middle class in a separate and unified political movement. But today and in the future this division will no longer obtain. Middle American political loyalties are ceasing to be torn between a left and a right that are increasingly convergent and indistinguishable. Aside from the ideological castration of the spokesmen of both sides in recent years, the main cause of the evanescence of right and left lies in the triumph of economic globalization.

The globalization of the American economy (and culture and population) not only presents a far more immediate threat to Middle American economic interests than the prospect of the libertarian and pro-business let-'em-eat-cake policies of the right but also strips the right of its capacity to appeal to Middle Americans at all. As champions of the globalist right like Jack Kemp, Phil Gramm, Steve Forbes, Newt Gingrich, Ben Wattenberg, George Gilder, Robert Bartley, Julian Simon, and George Will never tire of explaining, globalization means the disappearance of nationality, of cultures closely linked to national identity, probably of national sovereignty itself, and even of the distinctive populations of which nations are composed. By unequivocally signing on to globalization, then, the right has effectively metamorphosed itself into the left and forfeited the sole grounds of its appeal to the nationalism and social and cultural conservatism that continue to animate Middle Americans. The right may still thump its chest ferociously about crime and abortion, and its leaders may still thunder about sex and violence in movies they have never seen, but even on these issues the right's obsession with economic uplift as a panacea for crime, welfare, and moral decline serves to emasculate its older defense of national interests and cultural order. The only reason the Republican Party has not already jettisoned its anti-abortion positions and the only reason Bob Dole continues to complain about objectionable movies and TV programs is the influence of the large, militant, and well-organized "religious right," itself a Middle American movement though one that can never exert more than a limited appeal.

Having denuded itself of any reason for Middle Americans to support it, the right can no longer expect the Reagan Democrats to return to the Republican column. Given a choice between only the globalist right and the equally globalist and counter-cultural left, Middle Americans may well simply support the latter (they did so in 1992 by voting for Clinton over Bush), because at least the left can be expected to refrain from gutting the entitlement programs with which Middle American economic interests are so closely linked. The 1994 Republican congressional sweep was less a mandate for the GOP than a frenetic quest by alienated voters to attach themselves to some political entity that just might resist the Ruling Class and its regime and embrace the demands Middle Americans are calling for. There was little danger of that from "revolutionaries" like Mr. Gingrich, and in the past year or so the sprouting of militia groups, the land war in the Western states, the religious right itself, and the popularization of conspiracy theories that at least symbolically convey the hostility and hatred with which the popular mind regards the federal leviathan and the elites attached to it testify to the depth of the political and cultural alienation that now stalks through the nation.

While Buchanan rightly distances himself from the more bizarre and pathological expressions of Middle American unrest, no candidate in the fields of either party has so clearly enlisted himself with the central message of the Middle American revolt. His columns and commentary in the months prior to his announcement of his candidacy began developing an economic doctrine that radically departed from conventional conservative free-market and free-trade ideology, the main source of Middle American distaste for Republicans and the mainstream right. Buchanan continues to support economic deregulation, a flat tax, and the abolition of taxes on inheritances, family farms and businesses of less than $2 million, but in his last months as a commentator he devoted a series of columns to attacking the "myth of Economic Man" and formulating what he called "a conservatism of the heart" and "economic nationalism," pegged on his active opposition to NAFTA, GATT, the World Trade Organization, and the $50-billion Mexican Bail-Out.

The core of his economic message consists of a rejection of the thinly masked economic determinism that Kemp, Gramm, and Gingrich harbor and an affirmation of the primacy of cultural identity, national sovereignty, and national interests over narrowly economic goals and values. Increasingly, his economic nationalism seems to define and drive his whole candidacy, informing even his cultural conservatism, though the concept of "economic" implicit in his writing and speeches is considerably broader than conventional concepts of either the left or the right. "Economics," it should be recalled, derives from Greek words meaning "laws of the household," and the purpose of economic life in Buchanan's world-view is not simply to gain material satisfaction but to support families and the social institutions and identities that evolve from families as the fundamental units of human society and human action.

Thus, his "America First" foreign policy is more than the foreign policy isolationism preached by the old America First Committee and considerably more than the neo-isolationism supported today by most pro-free-trade paleo-libertarians. For Buchanan, "America First" implies not only putting U.S. national interests over those of other nations and abstractions like "world leadership," "global harmony," and the "New World Order," but also giving priority to the nation over the gratification of individual and subnational interests. Protectionism, to replace the federal taxes Buchanan would abolish and to "insulate the wages of U.S. workers from foreign laborers who must work for $1 an hour or less," follows from his formulation of economic nationalism, reflecting the economic interests and identity of the nation, just as a defense and foreign policy follows from his political nationalism, reflecting the political interests and identity of the nation. So, for that matter, does his support for curtailing, through a five-year moratorium, all immigration, legal as well as illegal, as a main pillar of his formulation of a cultural nationalism.

Buchanan's nationalism appears to break with the specter of individualism that has haunted American conservative ideology since the 1930s. It is based on the premise that the individual outside social and cultural institutions is an abstraction, and it probably shows Buchanan's debt to Catholic social theory rather than the atomistic and acquisitive egoism that descends from the libertarian right of John Locke. In one column, Buchanan supported the "humane economy" espoused by the Austrian School economist Wilhelm Röpke in contrast (not quite accurately, as I am told) to the acquisitive economic individualism of Ludwig von Mises. More recently, the *New York Times* quotes him as remarking,

> We have to ask ourselves as conservatives what it is we want to conserve in America. I believe in the market system, but I don't worship the market system. I don't worship at the altar of economic efficiency as I believe some so-called conservatives do. To prefer a 100,000-hog confinement to hundreds of family farms, it seems to me, is not conservatism. I mean, that's to worship as a

supermarket civilization.

Yet, while Buchanan's nationalism may tweak the noses of right-wing individualists, it also breaks significantly with the large-state nationalist tradition of Europe and American Hamiltonians, for whom the centralized national state defines and even creates the nation. Unlike liberal protectionists like Richard Gephardt, Buchanan explicitly seeks to use tariffs as substitutes for federal taxes, not as additional taxes. His campaign's official statement of principles explicitly endorses "restoration of the 10th Amendment," holding that "many functions of the federal government are, *de facto*, unconstitutional" (he might have added *de jure* as well) and encompassing abolition of major cabinet-level departments. He also calls for stripping federal judges of power through judicial term limits, "voter recall of renegade federal jurists," and eight-year reconfirmations of Supreme Court justices. For Buchanan, in contrast to large-state nationalists, the nation is fundamentally a social and cultural unit, not the creation of the state and its policies, but a continuing, organic body that transcends individuals and gives identity to itself through a common way of life and a common people. It is the national culture, embodied in the way of life and the people themselves, rather than the national state, that defines the nation, and hence cultural traditionalism is as central to Buchanan's nationalism as swollen statism is to European and Hamiltonian nationalists. The "cultural war" for Buchanan is not Republican swaggering about family values and dirty movies but a battle over whether the nation itself can continue to exist under the onslaught of the militant secularism, acquisitive egoism, economic and political globalism, demographic inundation, and unchecked state centralism supported by the Ruling Class.

Also unlike the conventional right, Buchanan does not confine his criticism of the Ruling Class to federal bureaucrats. Though he denies that he considers "big business an enemy," as he told Tom Carson of the *Village Voice* in Iowa, in a line he has repeated elsewhere, "I just think a lot of modern corporate capitalists — the managerial class basically — has no loyalty to any country anymore, or any particular values other than the bottom line." The remark points to a conception of the Ruling Class as fundamentally disengaged or deracinated from the nation and culture it dominates, and resembles similar views of 20th century ruling elites voiced by Joseph Schumpeter, the late Christopher Lasch, and James Burnham, among others.

Buchanan thus seems to share the perception that the fundamental polarity in American politics and culture today is between a deracinated and self-serving Ruling Class centered on but not confined to the central state, on the one hand, and Middle American groups, on the other, with the latter constituting both the economic core of the nation through their labor and productive skills as well as the culturally defining core that sustains the identity of the nation itself. The economic interests as well as the cultural habits and ideologies of the Ruling Class drive it toward globalization — the managed destruction of the nation, its sovereignty, its culture, and its people — while those of Middle Americans drive them toward support for and re-enforcement of the nation and its organic way of life. The implicit recognition of this polarity by the Buchanan campaign places him firmly on the side of Middle Americans more clearly than any other political figure in the country today.

The only figure who could rival him for that role is Ross Perot, but Perot's ideas, despite their focus on Middle Americans, are far less sophisticated, far less visionary, and far less radical than those of the former columnist and presidential speechwriter. Perot appears to have little grasp of the nature of the Ruling Class as a systemic entity, and his tirades against the central state never seem to rise above the level of grousing about corruption, incompetence, waste, and fraud. Perot seems to lack any perception of the structure of the state as problematic and confines his criticism merely to the abuse of the state structure. Buchanan's critique of the central state, at least implicitly, is shaped by his comprehension that the flaws of the state as it is presently structured derive from its control and exploitation by the Ruling Class, that the elites themselves are the real enemy and that the state, while far too large and intrusive, is simply their instrument. Control of the state by a social force or elite different from that of the forces that now control it could shape the state to support Middle American interests and values rather than crush them.

Hence, Buchanan not infrequently has rattled free-market anti-statist conservatives by his support for higher unemployment benefits for displaced workers, and last fall he tossed a brick at congressional Republicans who were insisting on cutting the growth of Medicare. "Instead of going after Medicare," Buchanan told New Hampshire factory workers, "we ought to start dealing with foreign aid, end those $50 billion bailouts, start dealing with the World Bank loan guarantees." He explained to the *Voice*'s Tom Carson that "I think government can fairly be used" to restructure tax incentives and penalties to discourage businesses from moving their operations overseas. Buchanan's anti-statism is genuine, but it rightly focuses on dismantling the present state as the present Ruling Class has constructed it; he does not purport to be an anarchist who imagines the state is an unnecessary and unmitigated evil, and "anarcho-libertarians" drawn to his America First foreign policy need to understand that Richard Nixon's former speechwriter would have no hesitation in making full use of the constitutionally legitimate powers of the federal government. They also need to understand that reducing the present leviathan to its constitutionally legitimate powers would not excite any but their most eccentric phobias of statism.

Neither the anti-statist right nor cultural conservatives have any good reason to be uncomfortable with the new identity Buchanan is building, though Economic Men like Kemp and Gramm and neoconservative apologists for the federal leviathan have plenty of reason to resist him and the new political horse he is saddling. If the anti-statists bridle at his protectionism, they will at least get the satisfaction of replacing much of the current tax structure of the state with tariffs, and the Old Right has long recognized that cultural and moral destruction is in large part driven by the swollen state and the powers of social management it has usurped in education, the arts, and the imperial federal judiciary. Buchanan explicitly vows to dismantle these parts of the leviathan, and given the Middle American social structure that today must underlie any serious political resistance to the federal mega-state and the Ruling Class it supports, the Old Right has no practical alternative anyway.

Yet, if Buchanan has one major flaw as a spokesman for and an architect of the new Middle American political identity that transcends and synthesizes both left and right, it is that he persistently exhibits a proclivity to draw back from the implications of his own radicalism. This penchant became evident in 1992, when he insisted on endorsing George Bush and even on campaigning for him, and last year he also vowed to support the Republican ticket even if he was not the nomi-nee. Any such commitment on Buchanan's part should be contingent on other candidates' commitment to support him if he is nominated, but so far none has bothered to do so. Buchanan, for all the implicit and often explicit radicalism of his ideas and campaign, remains deeply wedded to the Republican Party and to a conservative political label, and he tends to greet criticism of his deviations from conservative orthodoxy with affirmations of ideological doctrine. Last year, as conservative criticism of him began to flutter more fiercely, his re-sponse was that "The only area of disagreement I have [with tradi-tional conservatives] is trade, and that's crucial to bringing back the Perot voters" to the Republican Party.

Buchanan's loyalty to the GOP is perhaps touching, especially since almost no Republican leader or conservative pundit has much good to say about him, and the loudest mouths for the "Big Tent" are always the first to try to push him out of it. Even today, many Repub-licans try to blame the 1992 defeat of George Bush's inept and lacklus-ter bid for re-election on Buchanan's now-famous speech at the Hous-ton convention, a speech that was the only memorable event of the whole proceeding and which Buchanan himself continues to defend and even to distribute as literature for his present campaign. But, touching or not, Buchanan's refusal to break even more definitely with a conventional conservative identity and with a Republican Party whose leadership fears and despises him, his beliefs, and his followers is a serious error. I recall in late 1991, in the aftermath of a wall-to-wall gathering at his home to discuss his coming campaign, I told him privately that he would be better off without all the hangers-on, direct-mail artists, fund-raising whiz kids, marketing and PR czars, and the rest of the crew that today constitutes the backbone of all that remains of the famous "Conservative Movement" and who never fail to show up on the campaign doorstep to guzzle someone else's liquor and pocket other people's money. "These people are defunct," I told him. "You don't need them, and you're better off without them. Go to New Hampshire and call yourself a patriot, a nationalist, an America Firster, but don't even use the word 'conservative.' It doesn't mean anything any more."

Pat listened, but I can't say he took my advice. By making his bed with the Republicans, then and today, he opens himself to charges that he's not a "true" party man or a "true" conservative, constrains his chances for victory by the need to massage trunk-waving Republicans whose highest goal is to win elections, and only dilutes and deflects the radicalism of the message he and his Middle American Revolution have to offer. The sooner we hear that message loudly and clearly, without distractions from Conservatism, Inc., the Stupid Party, and their managerial elite, the sooner Middle America will be able to speak with an authentic and united voice, and the sooner we can get on with conserving the nation from the dominations and powers that are destroying it.

[March, 1996]

The Buchanan Victory

Whether a full-scale nuclear war between modern super-powers would last quite as long as the three-week blitzkrieg among this year's candidates for the Republican presidential nomination is an intriguing question that neither military nor political scientists seem to have asked, but whatever the answer, a duel with nuclear weapons might well be less bloodthirsty than the GOP's recent shoot-out at the OK Corral of American democracy. The philosopher Rousseau remarked that the English people were really free only once every seven years when they were allowed to vote for a new Parliament, and to judge from the foolishness, lies, and chicanery in which most of the leading Republican contenders engaged, Americans might be better off if we gave up the pretense of freedom entirely and contented ourselves with the benign and pacific oriental despotism of Suleiman the Magnificent.

The fraudulence of the Republican primaries was transparent from the first, with the most insipid of the candidates, Lamar Alexander, running around the country banging on a piano in his now-forgotten and increasingly malodorous plaid shirt. If the Republican rank-and-filers who had to endure his clowning had any self-respect, they would have pelted him from the podium with rotten fruit and dead cats for coming before them with his insults to their intelligence. But few of the other ne'er-do-wells who presented themselves for the mandate of the people's will were any better.

Yet the star of the Republican primaries, and most likely of the whole election, was Pat Buchanan, whose early victories seemed to promise a political revolution that would elevate American politics above the level of mind-numbing piano-playing and the triumph of high-rolling backstairs intrigue. Buchanan was by far the most interesting and the most substantive candidate the Republicans or the country had to offer, and for those Americans who have glimpsed the full depths of the depravity to which our political culture has sunk, it was no surprise that his early successes were greeted by the concerted onslaught of mendacity and character assassination that played a major role in turning his success into failure.

Buchanan's victory in New Hampshire elicited much the same mentality inside Washington, on both the right and the left, that must have prevailed in Paris when the Germans swung around the Maginot Line, and one can easily imagine such spokesdogs of the old order as Sam Donaldson and George Will hoofing it to Casablanca to wheedle for letters of transit to some safer climate.

The old order did not crumble, of course, but stood and fought with the only weapons it has left, and for the last two weeks of February and well into March, the court media raked up and rehearsed every conceivable flaw, foible, and florid passage remotely associated with Buchanan, from provocative sentences in his columns a decade earlier to confidential memoranda he had written for Richard Nixon in the early '70s to the schoolboy tricks he and his brothers may or may not have played on the neighbors of their parents in the 50s to the friends with whom he occasionally has dinner today to the way he pronounced supposed "codewords" like "Goldman Sachs." If the latter was part of a code, it's one that none but the Ruling Class itself understands, since most Americans probably thought Goldman Sachs was simply the name of a Manhattan department store.

Undoubtedly the smear-krieg was one of the principal reasons for Buchanan's subsequent loss; even if Republican voters didn't believe it, they knew it was only a foretaste of what would be unleashed if Buchanan won the nomination, and they also figured (perhaps inaccurately) that a nominee subjected to such a mendacious Niagara could not win the election. Since winning the election is the only principle the Stupid Party cares about any more, it seemed to follow that the harmless and decrepit Bob Dole rather than Buchanan should be the party's choice.

But there is another reason for Buchanan's failure besides the smear-krieg by left and right, and that has to do with a fundamental flaw of his campaign. That flaw was probably not the fault of the candidate himself, at least not in any sense larger than that the man in charge is always at fault for whatever goes wrong, and it may be a flaw that is inherent in the nature of any populist crusade of the right in contemporary American politics. But it remains a flaw, and it needs to be made clear to anyone who seeks to pick up the Buchanan mantle in the future.

Precisely because Buchanan chose to challenge the plutocratic power structure of American politics, he was never able to attract the high-dollar contributions from the plutocrats that constantly fed the campaigns of his rivals. As of the time of the Arizona primary, the turning point of the campaign, Buchanan had spent a total of about $10 million, compared to the $25 million spent by Mr. Dole and Malcolm S. "Steve" Forbes, Jr. Mr. Forbes, of course, spent his own money in order to avoid federal spending limits, and by doing so he was able simply to buy the Arizona primary, one of his few victories. Dole, Alexander, and even Phil Gramm, precisely because they mounted campaigns intended to serve the plutocracy, were able to pull far more money into their coffers and to deck out their campaigns with all the bells and whistles needed to make good Republicans believe that the candidates before them and the choices offered them are real.

Because of the financial limitations of the Buchanan campaign, Buchanan was unable to build the kind of organization he needed. His strategy from the first was to concentrate his whole effort on early states like Louisiana, Iowa, and New Hampshire, and in those states his organization was sound and his efforts were victorious. The problems arose immediately afterwards, when the lack of preparation in Arizona, South Carolina, and Georgia during the year before the primaries began to cause the campaign's bottom to fall out.

Not only was the campaign unprepared in those and other states but also Buchanan failed to make use of the issues that could have brought him grassroots votes there. He failed to make affirmative action a major theme in the South and continued to dwell on his opposition to free trade and abortion, issues that appealed only to special and limited constituencies. Perhaps most important, in South Carolina, he or his campaign or both managed to flub the Confederate Flag issue, one that could have brought him a clear victory on the eve of a bank of Southern primaries. The story behind the boondoggle exposes what was a further flaw in the psychology of the campaign.

For the last couple of years, the Confederate Flag that flies over the state Capitol in Columbia has been the center of a major state-wide controversy, with the NAACP, white liberals, and mainstream conservatives in the state demanding or condoning its removal. The flag has not been removed, in large part because one man, a local chiropractor named Bill Carter, successfully mobilized a grassroots crusade to keep the flag flying. Carter in 1992 was state chairman for David Duke's presidential campaign, a fact well known in the state and to the local Buchanan campaign when it appointed Carter to its steering committee this year.

But when the Larry Pratt affair broke just before the New Hampshire primary, the South Carolina Buchanan campaign told Carter he had to be dropped from the committee because of his ties to Duke. Indeed, despite Buchanan's own magnificently principled and courageous public expressions of support for Pratt, who had spoken before some rather bizarre groups on the right, the campaign immediately seems to have started an internal purge of former Duke supporters and other workers who had even the slightest "links" to the out-of-the-mainstream right.

But in South Carolina, the Buchanan campaign managed to alien-

ate Carter and his followers, who consist of some 45,000 names. Carter
had already started mobilizing this following for Buchanan and preparing mass mailings to get his people into the voting booths when the
Buchanan campaign chucked him out. Buchanan himself, in Arizona
at the time, was quoted in the South Carolina press as saying his campaign "had no room for racists or those connected to racist organizations." Whether this remark was consciously aimed at Carter or whether
the local press merely played it that way remains unclear.

But what is clear is that by alienating Carter, Buchanan muffed the
Confederate Flag issue in the state. Carter did send out some 9,000
pieces of mail urging voters in the state's third congressional district to
vote for Buchanan, and two of the five counties in the district were the
only ones Buchanan carried in the state. But had Carter sent out the full
mailing, which he could not do without help from the campaign, Buchanan might have won similar results across South Carolina. As Carter
himself wrote in a subsequent op-ed, "Without ever having met me or
knowing anything about me, Buchanan was polishing his own image
in the press at my expense.... What chance does a little guy like me
have to be heard or have his say?"

It's doubtful that either Buchanan or his national campaign was
trying to harm Carter, but that may have been the result. It's more
likely that the smear-krieg mounted by the national press in the week
before was affecting the campaign, certainly at the local and perhaps at
the national levels. The campaign's immediate response to the charges
of "racism" and "racist" associates and workers was one of denial,
escape, and evasion and a noticeable muting of themes that might be
interpreted as catering to "racism."

But the blunt truth is that there can be no serious national campaign of the Populist Right without former Duke supporters, militia
members, and other inhabitants of the margins of national politics, and
it is not possible to organize a real campaign without them. Those who
lead and run a populist campaign of the right have to face that truth and
to figure out how to deal with it when confronted with their "links" to

such "extremists." They can do what the Buchanan campaign did, which was to purge the marginal elements and curl up in denial, or they can go on the offense, exposing how the Ruling Class and its pet media use charges of "racism" and "extremism" to delegitimize and suppress any challenge to their power from the right. If they do the former, they will merely reconfirm the legitimacy of the imposed political boundaries; if they do the latter, they will retain their own support intact and use the occasion for a further challenge to the powers they claim to be opposing.

The Buchanan failure was a failure to follow through on the radicalism his campaign had originally promised, and it suggests that the radical implications of the campaign remain unclear in the minds of those who designed and managed the campaign, that the campaign sought to keep at least one foot firmly in the camp of conservative Republicanism and was unable or unwilling to step outside the camp into the new identity it promised to create.

Yet these were tactical failures of execution, and it would be a serious error to dwell on them too much at the expense of the larger strategic victory the Buchanan campaign won, despite its failure to capture the Republican nomination. The strategic victory of the Buchanan campaign lies in the fact that Buchanan pretty clearly destroyed the political pretenses of both neo-conservatism and the mainstream right and replaced them with his own nationalist, populist, and Middle American paradigm. The important fact about the Buchanan campaign of 1996 is that Buchanan steadily won second place throughout the early contests, when he faced several better-funded and better-organized campaigns with far more establishment support. It was to those other banners that neo-conservatives and the Beltway Right flocked. Their first choices — Jack Kemp, Dan Quayle, Bill Bennett, Dick Cheney — could not even mount campaigns. Their second-level choice, Phil Gramm, could not make it to the first primary. Bennett then signed on with Alexander and was shot out of the skies a few weeks later. Kemp then went with Forbes and followed Bennett into oblivion.

The clear lesson is that neither neo-conservatism nor the Beltway Right (in so far as they are at all distinguishable) can any longer command a significant political following at the grassroots level; only Buchanan or a movement espousing his ideas can do so, and the hatred and fury with which his early success was greeted shows that the Ruling Class knows this. It also must know that its age of dominance is coming to an end and that in its last days it has no better defense than to rely on the kind of repression that it visited upon the man who has shaken its foundations more than any other in the last quarter century. For all the flaws and uncertainties of the Buchanan campaign, it would be a mistake for either the friends or the foes of the movement Buchanan has created and mobilized to imagine that the king's men can ever put the Ruling Class and its old order back together again. What its friends must do now is understand how to build on their real victories and to avoid the tactical errors that helped thwart the completion of its victory.

[June, 1996]

About the Author

Born in 1947 in Chattanooga, Tennessee, Samuel Francis earned his B.A. from Johns Hopkins University, and his M.A. and Ph.D. in modern history from the University of North Carolina at Chapel Hill.

He was a policy analyst at the Heritage Foundation in Washington, D.C., specializing in foreign affairs, terrorism, intelligence, and national security issues. He worked as a legislative assistant for national security affairs to the late U.S. Senator John P. East (Republican, North Carolina).

After leaving Capitol Hill he joined the *Washington Times* where he was deputy assistant editorial page editor and a staff columnist. In 1989 and 1990, he received the Distinguished Writing Award for Editorial Writing from the American Society of Newspaper Editors.

Dr. Francis is the author of several articles and studies on terrorism, including *The Soviet Strategy of Terror* (1981; revised edition 1985). He has published articles or reviews in a number of newspapers and magazines including the *New York Times*, *U.S.A. Today*, *National Review*, and *Chronicles: A Magazine of American Culture*, of which he is a contributing editor.

He is also a member of the national board of directors of the Council of Conservative Citizens, and the board of editorial advisors for *Modern Age: A Quarterly Review*.

He is the author of two previous books, *Power and History: The Political Thought of James Burnham* (1984) and *Beautiful Losers: Essays on the Failure of American Conservatism* (1993).

Since 1991 Dr. Francis has written a twice-weekly newspaper column syndicated nationally by Tribune Media Services, and he publishes his own newsletter, *The Samuel Francis Letter*.

ORDER FORM

For additional copies of
Revolution from the Middle
by Samuel Francis

Name:_____

Address:_____

_____

City/State/Zip_____

All prices include postage and handling
charges to one address.

☐   1 copy $6.95
☐   2-19 copies $5.00 each
☐   20 or more copies $3.00 each

Total number of copies ordered _____= $_____
Please make checks payable to: Middle American Press
(N.C. residents please add 6% sales tax)

Mail this form (or a copy) to:
Middle American Press
P.O. Box 17088
Raleigh, NC 27619

We will be happy to send *Revolution from the Middle* directly to your
friends. Please enclose the name and address of the person to receive the
book as well as payment of $6.95 for each name listed.

Subscribe to

Middle America's Monthly Newspaper

☐ YES! Enter my one-year (12 issues) risk-free subscription to *Middle American News* at the special subscription rate of only $15.00. (2 years for $27.00)

☐ Enclosed is my check or money order. I understand I may cancel at any time within four months for a full refund.

Name_____

Address_____

_____

City/State/Zip_____

Please allow up to 5 weeks for delivery of first issue.

**Mail to: M.A.N.
            Subscription Department
            P.O. Box 17088
            Raleigh, NC 27619**

Please make checks payable to M.A.N.
Sorry, no credit cards or "bill me" orders accepted.